Student Applications Book

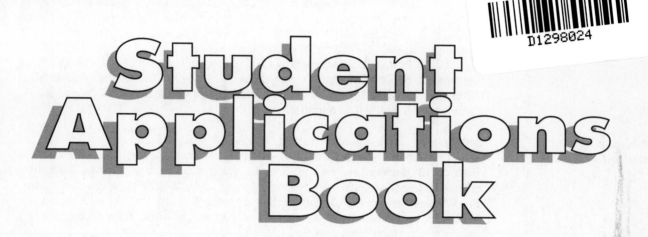

Great Source Education Group
a Houghton Mifflin Company
Wilmington, Massachusetts

www.greatsource.com

AUTHORS

Jim Burke
Author

Burlingame High School, Burlingame, California
Jim Burke, author of *Reading Reminders: Tools, Tips, and Techniques* and *The English Teacher's Companion,* has taught high school English for 13 years. His most recent books, *Tools for Thought* and *Illuminating Texts: How to Teach Students to Read the World,* further explore reading and those strategies that can help all students succeed in high school. He was the recipient of the California Reading Association's Hall of Fame Award in 2001 and the Conference on English Leadership's Exemplary English Leadership Award in 2000. He currently serves on the National Board of Professional Teaching Standards for English Language Arts.

Ron Klemp
Contributing Author

Los Angeles Unified School District, Los Angeles, California
Ron Klemp is the Coordinator of Reading for the Los Angeles Unified School District. He has taught Reading, English, and Social Studies and was a middle school Dean of Discipline. He is also a coordinator/facilitator at the Secondary Practitioner Center, a professional development program in the Los Angeles Unified School District. He has been teaching at California State University, Cal Lutheran University, and National University.

Wendell Schwartz
Contributing Author

Adlai Stevenson High School, Lincolnshire, Illinois
Wendell Schwartz has been a teacher of English for 36 years. For the last 24 years he also has served as the Director of Communication Arts at Adlai Stevenson High School. He has taught gifted middle school students for the last 12 years, as well as teaching graduate-level courses for National Louis University in Evanston, Illinois.

Editorial:
Design:
Illustrations:

Developed by Nieman, Inc. with Phil LaLeike
Ronan Design: Christine Ronan, Sean O'Neill, Maria Mariottini, Victoria Mullins
Mike McConnell

Printed in the United States of America

International Standard Book Number: 0-669-49508-5
(Student Applications Book)

2 3 4 5 6 7 8 9—DBH—10 09 08 07 06 05

International Standard Book Number: 0-669-49513-1
(Student Applications Book, Teacher's Edition)

1 2 3 4 5 6 7 8 9—DBH—10 09 08 07 06 05 04 03

Table of Contents for Student Applications Book

Lessons

What Is Reading? 6

Why You Read 8

What You Read 9

The Reading Process 10

Essential Reading Skills 12

Reading Actively
    from *Driver's Ed* by Caroline B. Cooney 15

Reading Paragraphs
    from "Rothschild's Fiddle" by Anton Chekhov 17

Reading History
    from "Mesoamerican Civilization and the Olmec" 20

Reading Science
    "The Immune System" 31

Reading Math
    "Surface Area of a Prism" 40

Focus on Foreign Language
    "Los Verbos *Ser* y *Estar*" 48

Focus on Science Concepts
    "Inflammatory Response" 50

Focus on Study Questions
    The Protestant Reformation 53

Focus on Word Problems
    Computer Auto-save 55

Reading a Personal Essay
    from "Pleasure Boat Studio" by Ou-Yang Hsiu 57

Reading an Editorial
    "Let Us Reason Together" by W. E. B. DuBois 65

Reading a News Story
"Two Inmates Vanish from Alcatraz" 74

Reading a Biography
from *Spotted Tail* by Charles A. Eastman...84

Reading a Memoir
from *When the Sea-Asp Stings* by Irvin S. Cobb...94

Focus on Persuasive Writing
"Eastern Ballet Bankruptcy: What You Can Do" 105

Focus on Speeches
from "Child Labor and Women's Suffrage" by Florence Kelley 107

Reading a Short Story
"The Voyage" by Katherine Mansfield 110

Reading a Novel
from *Tarzan of the Apes* by Edgar Rice Burroughs 124

Focus on Plot
"Pegasus and the Chimaera" by Thomas Bulfinch.....................................137

Focus on Setting
from "Death of a Traveling Salesman" by Eudora Welty 139

Focus on Characters
from *Song of Solomon* by Toni Morrison 141

Focus on Theme
from *Lord of the Flies* by William Golding...143

Focus on Dialogue
from "The Golden Honeymoon" by Ring Lardner...146

Focus on Comparing and Contrasting
from *A Tale of Two Cities* by Charles Dickens
and from *The Garden of Eden* by Ernest Hemingway 148

Reading a Poem
"The Charge of the Light Brigade" by Alfred, Lord Tennyson...........................150

Focus on Language
"The Lake Isle of Innisfree" by William Butler Yeats....................................157

Focus on Meaning
"After Death" by Christina Rossetti 160

Focus on Sound and Structure
from "The Bells" by Edgar Allan Poe...162

Reading a Play
    from *A Doll's House* by Henrik Ibsen 165

Focus on Language
    from *A Doll's House* by Henrik Ibsen 175

Focus on Theme
    from *A Doll's House* by Henrik Ibsen 178

Focus on Shakespeare
    from *The Merchant of Venice* by William Shakespeare...........................180

Reading a Website
    www.moviemania.movies.com 182

Reading a Graphic
    "Transportation Trends: Vehicles per U.S. Household" 190

Reading a Driver's Handbook
    "Passing Another Vehicle" 198

Focus on Reading Instructions 205

Focus on Reading for Work
    Sick Leave Policy 207

Reading Tests and Test Questions
    from *Krik? Krak!* by Edwidge Danticat 210

Focus on English Tests 217

Focus on Writing Tests 220

Focus on Standardized Tests 222

Focus on History Tests 224

Focus on Math Tests 227

Focus on Science Tests 229

Learning New Words
    from *Fahrenheit 451* by Ray Bradbury...231

Skills for Learning New Words
    from *The Return of the King* by J. R. R. Tolkien.....................................233

Dictionary Dipping 235

Focus on Using a Thesaurus..236

Analogies 237

Author and Title Index 240

What Is  Reading?

Practice makes perfect, and this is especially true when it comes to reading. The more you read—and think about what you read—the more you will comprehend and remember.

Reading is . . .

You can train yourself to be a good reader, just as an athlete trains to become a champion. First, think about reading. Ask yourself, "What does reading mean to me?"

Directions: Reread pages 26–27 in your *Reader's Handbook*. Then write your reactions to the following sentences.

Understanding Reading

Reading Is . . .	My Thoughts
working	
thinking	
imagining	
reacting	
enjoying	

NAME ....

FOR USE WITH PAGES 26–27

How I feel about reading

The *Reader's Handbook* can help you read better. It also can improve your enjoyment of a text.

Directions: Write your thoughts and feelings about reading on the lines below. Return to this page at the end of the year to find out how your feelings have changed.

This is how I feel about reading:

....

....

....

....

This is what I find easiest about reading:

....

....

....

This is what I find hardest:

....

....

....

....

Why You  Read

The purpose of this book is to improve your reading skills. Before you turn another page, however, you need to think about your reasons for reading.

Reasons for reading

The *Reader's Handbook* describes several good reasons for reading. But surely you have a few reasons of your own.

Directions: Read or reread pages 27–28 in the *Reader's Handbook*. Summarize the reasons for reading. Then name a reason of your own.

Reasons for Reading

1. Academic reading: ....

....

....

2. Personal reading: ....

....

....

3. Workplace reading: ....

....

....

4. Functional reading: ....

....

.... **Summarize what the handbook says about these reasons for reading.** ....

My reason: ....

....

....

....

What You 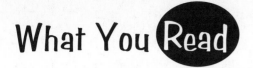Read

Think of all the things that you read in a given day. You may be surprised to learn that you read something almost every minute of every hour.

Kinds of reading

Sometimes you read for school. Sometimes you read for pleasure. But often you read without even knowing it.

Directions: Make a list of everything you've read in the last 24 hours. Then compare your list with a classmate's.

My Reading List

1.
2.
3.
4.
5.
6.
7.
8.
9.
10.
11.
12.
13.
14.

The Reading Process

The reading process is the steps you follow to read, understand, relate to, and remember a text. Good readers have an individual reading process that allows them to fully comprehend what they read.

Your reading process

You have your own habits and rituals when it comes to reading. Think about them for a moment. What do you do before, during, and after reading?

Directions: Explain your reading process on the lines below.

Before Reading

....

....

....

During Reading

....

....

....

After Reading

....

....

....

The handbook's reading process

The *Reader's Handbook* describes a reading process that will help you get *more* from a text. Think of it as a road map. It can point you in the right direction before you open a book and prevent you from getting lost once you start reading.

Directions: Read pages 38–43 in the *Reader's Handbook*. Then summarize the reading process on the lines below.

Before Reading

....
....
....
....
....
....

During Reading

....
....
....
....

After Reading

....
....
....
....

Essential Reading Skills

You already have tons of reading skills. The key is to figure out how to use them. As a first step, sharpen these essential thinking skills: making inferences, drawing conclusions, comparing and contrasting, and evaluating.

Thinking Skill 1: Making Inferences

No writer will tell you everything. That's why it's important to make inferences—reasonable guesses—about what is going on in a text.

Directions: Read this paragraph. Then make inferences about what's happening, and fill out the chart.

Sample Paragraph

A mother, grandmother, and three children pile into the family van. The mother and grandmother wear sunhats and sunglasses; the three children wear visors. In the trunk is a picnic basket filled with sandwiches, sodas, and other lunch treats. The grandmother holds in her lap a straw bag that contains sunblock, lip balm, and ear drops. All of the children have buckets, shovels, and large towels. The children poke each other with the shovels, tell jokes, and sing songs. The mother and grandmother chat contentedly in the front seat.

My Inferences

The family is going to

I know this because:

What time of day is the family leaving their house?

I know this because:

How does the family feel about the trip?

I know this because:

Thinking Skill 2: Drawing Conclusions

Drawing conclusions means collecting information and then deciding what it means.

Directions: Read the facts in the left-hand column. Write your conclusions in the right-hand column.

Drawing Conclusions

Facts	My Conclusion
The mother and grandmother wear sunhats and sunglasses.	
In the trunk is a picnic basket filled with sandwiches, soda, and other lunch treats.	
All of the children have buckets, shovels, and large towels.	
The children poke each other, tell jokes, and sing songs.	

Thinking Skill 3: Comparing and Contrasting

Comparing means noting similarities between two or more things. Contrasting means exploring the differences.

Directions: Place two textbooks on your desk. Compare them in terms of size, shape, thickness, and appearance. Write your findings on the following Venn Diagram.

Write notes that describe Book A here.

Write notes that describe Book B here.

Title: ....

Title: ....

Write what they have in common here.

Thinking Skill 4: Evaluating

Evaluating is making a judgment. For example, you say why you did or did not like a book, or you consider whether an argument is valid or a news story you are evaluating is well written.

Directions: Think about two of the classes you took last year in school. Tell which you think was more interesting. Then explain your evaluation.

I would say .... was more interesting than ....

because ....

....

Reading Actively

Active readers stay involved. They ask questions, make predictions, and connect what they are reading to their own lives.

Ways of Reading Actively

Here are six ways of reading actively. Use them to help you get more from a text.

1. Mark or highlight

2. Ask questions

3. Clarify

4. React and connect

5. Visualize

6. Predict

Directions: Read this excerpt from a novel. Then complete the sticky notes.

from *Driver's Ed* by Caroline B. Cooney

Morgan kept a *Car and Driver* with him at all times, memorizing, studying, and yearning.

He had stood on the threshold of being sixteen ever since he could remember. He ached to be the driver. He wanted long journeys. Total freedom. Complete control. He'd leave town, leave the state, drive every turnpike in the nation from start to finish.

He had no destinations. He didn't care about destinations. He just wanted to drive. Fast.

1. Mark

Highlight any key information about the setting and the characters.

2. Question

Ask a question about Morgan.

from *Driver's Ed* by Caroline B. Cooney, continued

He came from a family that specialized in yearning for things.

His father yearned for power and was going to try to move up in the world: from statehouse to governor. His mother yearned for money and had just become full partner in her law firm. His sister, Starr, yearned for both these things, but she called it popularity.

3. React

Explain your reaction to the writing.

....

....

....

....

4. Predict

Predict some of the problems Morgan will have in this novel.

....

....

....

....

....

....

....

5. Visualize

Make a sketch of the scene here.

6. Clarify

Write your inferences about Morgan here.

....

....

....

....

....

Reading Paragraphs

Every paragraph has a subject and main idea. Your job as the reader is to find the subject and understand what the author has to say about it.

Step 1: Read the paragraph.

Directions: Read this paragraph from a short story. Highlight interesting details. Then write your thoughts on the sticky notes.

from "Rothschild's Fiddle" by Anton Chekhov

It was a small town, more wretched than a village, and almost all the inhabitants were old folk with a depressingly low death rate. Nor were many coffins required at the hospital and jail. In a word, business was bad. Had Jacob Ivanov been making coffins in a country town he would probably have owned a house and been called "mister." But in this dump he was plain Jacob, his street nickname was "Bronze" for whatever reason, and he lived as miserably as any farm laborer in his little old one-roomed shack which housed himself, his Martha, a stove, a double bed, coffins, his workbench, and all his household goods.

Highlight/Mark

What repeated words did you notice?

What important phrases or sentences did you highlight?

Question

Ask yourself a question about the main idea of this paragraph.

My question:

Step 2: Find the subject of the paragraph.

To find the subject of a paragraph, ask yourself, "What is this paragraph about?" Check the following places for clues about the subject:

Subject Checklist

☐ the title

☐ the first sentence

☐ any key words or repeated words and names

☐ the last sentence

Directions: Answer the following question about the paragraph you just read.

What is the "Rothschild's Fiddle" paragraph mostly about?

....

....

....

Step 3: Find the main idea of the paragraph.

The main idea is what the author is trying to say about the subject.

Stated Main Idea In some paragraphs, the author will state the main idea directly.

Directions: Reread the paragraph from "Rothschild's Fiddle." Look for a main idea sentence. Then complete the formula.

(Chekhov's subject)   (What he says about the subject)

Jacob's coffin-making business   + ...

(His main idea)

= ....

Implied Main Idea Sometimes the main idea of a paragraph is only implied. This means you'll need to infer, or make reasonable guesses about, the author's main idea. You do this by asking yourself, "What is the writer trying to tell me about the subject?"

Directions: Answer these questions about the paragraph.

What is Chekhov trying to tell you about Jacob and his coffin-making business?

How do you know this?

Step 4: Find support for the main idea.

Use a Main Idea Organizer to help you see how the main idea and supporting details work together in a paragraph.

Directions: Complete this organizer. Refer to your notes to help you.

◄ **Main Idea Organizer**

Subject		
Detail 1	**Detail 2**	**Detail 3**

Main Idea

Reading  History

History textbooks are full of names, dates, people, places, and ideas. Your job is to determine—and then memorize— the most important facts presented in each chapter.

Before Reading

Use the reading process and the strategy of note-taking to help you read a history chapter called "Mesoamerican Civilization and the Olmec."

 A **Set a Purpose**

Historians are like newspaper reporters. They focus on finding answers to six questions: *who, what, where, when, why,* and *how.*

- **Set your purpose by asking the 5 W's and H questions about the chapter.**

Directions: Use this 5 W's and H Organizer to write your purpose questions for reading "Mesoamerican Civilization and the Olmec."

5 W's and H Organizer

Who	What	Where	When	Why	How

B Preview

It's important to carefully preview a history chapter, especially if you're unfamiliar with the subject. Look at the title, the study guide or goals box, the first and last paragraphs, and any background information. Also pay attention to repeated or boldface words.

Directions: Preview the sample history chapter that follows. Write your ideas on the sticky notes.

Preview Notes

Textbooks

What is the title of the chapter? What is it mostly about?

What did you notice in the study guide box?

What did you learn from the first and last paragraphs?

What repeated and boldface terms did you notice?

NAME ....

FOR USE WITH PAGES 73–87

Chapter 11

Mesoamerican Civilization and the Olmec

Key Terms and Concepts
● ● ● ● ● ● ● ● ● ● ●
Mesoamerica
pre-Columbian
La Venta
San Lorenzo
nonegalitarian
elite
commoners
jade
cultivating

Goals

As you read, look for answers to these questions:
1. Who were the Olmec and when did they live?
2. In what ways did the Olmec learn to adapt to their environment?
3. What effect did trading have on the Olmec and nearby civilizations?

No study of **Mesoamerica** (a region extending south and east from central Mexico to include parts of Guatemala, Belize, Honduras, and Nicaragua) is complete without a thorough analysis of the Olmec, a complex **pre-Columbian** empire that managed to set the stage for all Mexican and Central American Indian empires in existence before Christopher Columbus arrived in America.

Even so, it is only within the last century or so that historians have been able to piece together what appears to be an accurate picture of the Olmec. What they have discovered is that the Olmec, despite severe hardship, managed to create one of the most mysterious and fascinating of the ancient worlds.

Stop and Think: Who and When

Who were the Olmec, and when did they live? Write your answers on the 5 W's and H Organizer on page 26.

Olmec Beginnings

Historians believe that the Olmec civilization developed around 1200 B.C. The Olmec people lived in the hot and humid lowlands of the Tuxtla Mountains in what are now the southern states of Veracruz and Tabasco in Mexico. The two major centers of the Olmec, **La Venta** and **San Lorenzo,** were located on rivers whose tributaries fed into the Gulf of Mexico.

Although this area of the world is lush and green, the early Olmec suffered grave hardships. Their biggest challenge was the pelting rainstorms that occurred throughout the year. Another challenge came in the form of the land, which the Olmec had to cultivate to survive. The region was mostly swampland and jungle and proved difficult to clear and even harder to farm. Planting crops was a nightmarish cycle of sowing seeds and then watching them wash away in punishing floods.

The Olmec people lived in the densest of jungles, which is why their ruins remained hidden for so many centuries.

Stop and Think: Where and What

Where did the Olmec live? What was their early life like?
Record your notes on the 5 W's and H Organizer on page 26.

Adaptation and Progress

Still, the Olmec people found ways to adapt to their environment. They learned to plant seeds deep into the rich soil along the riverbanks so they didn't wash away in the storms. They developed a kind of growing calendar that they could use to keep track of the seasons and know the best times of the year to plant and harvest the corn, beans, and squash that were the staple in their diet. They used this same calendar to plan different hunting seasons for the wild deer, pigs, pheasants, and monkeys that traveled through the jungle.

Stop and Think: How

How did the Olmec overcome challenges in farming and land cultivation?
Jot down your answers on the 5 W's and H Organizer on page 26.

In addition to learning how to adapt, the Olmec clearly placed a high value on progress. Historians have suggested that the Olmec—more than any other Mesoamerican civilization—made improvements in almost every aspect of their lives, from housing to fishing to their system of government. It is believed that the Olmec developed the first large-scale Mesoamerican trading network. For the first time ever, people who lived thousands of miles from each other were able to trade goods and share ideas and beliefs. The Olmec capitalized on what they learned and in turn influenced other civilizations to embrace the arts, politics, and religion of the Olmec people.

Olmec Society

At its height, the Olmec population was made up of tens of thousands of people and covered a distance as large as 7,000 square miles. Historians believe that the Olmec culture was **nonegalitarian,** which means that it was unequal in terms of political, social, and economic advantages.

Within Olmec society there were two classes of people: the **elite,** or upper class, and the **commoners,** or lower class. Olmec rulers, who were known as priest-kings, were believed to be direct descendants of the gods.

Historians have found evidence that the Olmec worshiped at least fourteen gods, although there may have been more. The most important Olmec god was a kind of jaguar-man who represented the mystery of life and death. The Olmec prayed to this god for safety from harm and good health for their children.

As a way of celebrating the jaguar-man and their other gods, the Olmec created huge stone monuments and at least one ceremonial center, which was located in La Venta. It was at this ceremonial center that the Olmec people prayed, sacrificed, and made generous offerings of **jade,** a highly prized mineral that the Indians of the region used for trading.

In the late 1800s, a huge head that was over seven feet tall and weighed close to three tons was unearthed in southern Mexico. It is believed that the Olmec sculpted these heads as monuments to their priest-kings.

The Arts

Although the primary business of the Olmec was farming and trading, it appears that these ancient peoples also placed a tremendous value on **cultivating** the arts, specifically architecture and sculpture. Archeologists have unearthed hundreds and hundreds of highly intricate Olmec carvings, monuments, and statues. Even more important, the Olmec created a huge number of stone tablets that are covered both back and front with hieroglyphics. These tablets have provided archeologists and historians with innumerable clues about the Olmec way of life.

Stop and Think: Why

Why do you suppose the Olmec were so interested in cultivating the arts?
Write the answers on the 5 W's and H Organizer on page 26.

The End of an Empire

No one is exactly sure what happened to the Olmec. Their hieroglyphics indicate that the Olmec had a keen understanding of weaponry and the strategies of war, so many historians have theorized that neighboring tribes banded together and defeated the Olmec in a war or series of wars around 400 B.C.

It's possible that these invading armies took as their prize the valuable trade routes the Olmec had established and made them their own. This competition for resources may have brought about the ruin of the Olmec and their advanced society.

Plan

It's up to you what strategy to use when reading a history chapter. Most readers, however, find that note-taking is an excellent choice.

- **Note-taking can help you process and remember what you've learned from a history chapter.**

Textbooks

During Reading

D Read with a Purpose

Remember that your reading purpose is to find answers to the following questions: *who, what, where, when, why,* and *how*.

Directions: Now do a careful reading of the history chapter. Make notes on this 5 W's and H Organizer as you read.

5 W's and H Organizer

The Olmec

Who	What	When

Where	How

Why do you suppose the Olmec were so interested in cultivating the arts?

Using the Strategy

There are all kinds of reading tools that work well with the strategy of note-taking. Two of these tools are shown on pages 80–81 of the *Reader's Handbook.*

Directions: Use the organizer below to create Key Word or Topic Notes for the text.

Key Word or Topic Notes

Write key words of your own here.

Write notes from the chapter here.

Key Words or Topics	My Notes

Textbooks

Understanding How History Chapters Are Organized

Most history chapters open with a study guide or goals box. It's important that you be able to define each term and answer every question in this box.

• **Use the study guide or goals box to help you figure out what's most important in the chapter.**

Directions: Return to the goals box on page 22. Answer the questions and define the terms.

1. Who were the Olmec, and when did they live?
....

....

....

2. In what ways did the Olmec learn to adapt to their environment?
....

....

....

3. What effect did trading have on the Olmec and nearby civilizations?
....

....

....

Define these terms:

Mesoamerica— ....

pre-Columbian— ....

La Venta and San Lorenzo— ....

nonegalitarian— ....

elite— ....

commoners— ....

jade— ....

cultivating— ....

E Connect

Making a personal connection to a textbook chapter or article can make history "come alive."

- **Imagining yourself a part of history can help you make a strong connection to what you've read.**

Directions: Imagine you lived with the Olmec. What would be the best thing about your life, and what would you find most challenging?

The best part of my life would be

....

because

....

The hardest part would be   because

....

....

Textbooks

After Reading

After you finish, think about what you've learned.

F Pause and Reflect

Reflect on your original reading purpose.

- **Ask yourself important questions about your purpose and what you've learned.**

Directions: Answer these three questions about the reading.

1. Did I meet the reading purpose I set in the beginning?

....

2. Do I know the answers to the 5 W's and H questions?

....

3. Could I discuss the chapter intelligently?

....

G Reread

Get into the habit of doing two careful readings of every textbook chapter. The additional time this takes will be well spent.

- **Use graphic organizers to help you get *more* from your second reading.**

Directions: Use this Web to help you group important facts and details from the Olmec chapter.

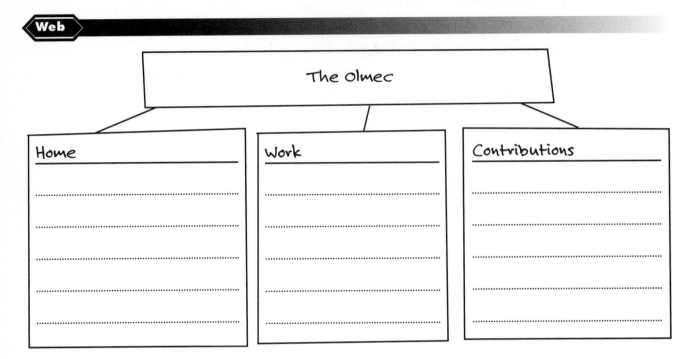

Web

The Olmec

Home	Work	Contributions

 H **Remember**

Good readers remember what they've read.

• **Conducting an "interview" about the subject can help you remember what you've read.**

Directions: Write three interview questions on the lines below. Then exchange books and have a partner answer them.

Question 1 ....

Answer 1 ....

Question 2 ....

Answer 2 ....

Question 3 ....

Answer 3 ....

NAME

Reading Science

To do well in science class, you have to make sense of the textbook. This means you need to understand the explanations, follow the instructions, and memorize the specialized vocabulary that is defined. The reading process can help.

Before Reading

Use what you've learned about reading textbooks to help you read and respond to a chapter on the human immune system.

 Set a Purpose

Your purpose when reading a science chapter is to learn everything you can about the subject.

> • **To set your purpose, turn the title of the chapter into a question.**

Directions: Write your purpose for reading "The Immune System" on the lines below. Then write what you expect to learn from the chapter.

My purpose: ....

....

Here are three things I expect to learn from this chapter:

1. ....

2. ....

3. ....

B Preview

Previewing is particularly important if the subject of the chapter is unfamiliar to you. Watch for items on this checklist:

Preview Checklist

☐ any headings

☐ any boxed items

☐ any boldface words or repeated words

☐ the first and last paragraphs

☐ any photos, maps, or diagrams

Directions: Skim the science chapter that follows. Place a check mark beside the features you noticed during your preview. Then make notes on the Preview Chart.

Preview Chart

The titles and headings tell me . . .	I noticed these boldface words . . .

The Immune System

The art tells me . . .	I expect to learn . . .

NAME ....

Chapter 11.3 The Immune System

> **Study Guide** **Objectives**
> • Learn the three types of immunity and how they work.
> • Understand how the body uses the immune system to fight disease.
>
> **Terms to Know**
>
> immunity   active immunity   pathogens   antibodies
> artificial active   passive immunity   macrophages   antigen
> immunity

You Need to Know...

1ST LINE OF DEFENSE: Physical barriers

2ND LINE OF DEFENSE: Inflammatory response

3RD LINE OF DEFENSE: The immune system

Did you have chicken pox or the measles when you were little? If so, you'll never have these diseases again because your body has built an immunity to them. **Immunity** is the body's ability to recognize and resist infection by specific pathogens or toxins.

Three Types of Immunity

When scientists talk about immunity, they do so in terms of three different types: active, artificial active, and passive immunity. **Active immunity** takes place when your body develops its own line of defense against particular **pathogens** to which you have been exposed. Your body does this by producing what are called **antibodies**, which can destroy pathogens. For example, if you are infected with chicken pox, your body will develop an active immunity to pathogens that cause the disease.

Artificial active immunity occurs when a vaccination is given. When you receive a vaccine, dead or weakened pathogens are introduced into your body, usually in the form of an injection or serum (see Figure 11.9). In response, your body produces antibodies against these pathogens.

Figure 11.9
In 1796, British physician Edward Jenner discovered that the cowpox virus (vaccinia) could protect humans against smallpox. Twenty-five years later, the artist Constant Desbordes painted this picture of a baby being vaccinated against the disease.

Passive immunity occurs when antibodies are produced by another source—either human or animal—and then transferred into your body. For example, if a doctor suspects that you may have a disease called tetanus, you will be injected with blood serum from an animal such as a pig or horse that has developed an immunity to that disease. Another example of passive immunity is the transfer of antibodies that occurs between mother and fetus.

Stop and Organize

Make notes in the first section of your Outline on page 36.

Macrophages and Antigens

Your body develops immunity by producing **macrophages,** which are gigantic white blood cells that engulf and then destroy pathogens. Macrophages alert the body that a pathogen is present. The process of engulfing the pathogen sends a signal to the body that the immune system needs to kick into high gear.

Macrophages must be very selective in which particles they engulf. They can tell which particles belong in the body by chemically recognizing the presence of antigens. An **antigen** is any foreign substance that can cause an immune response. In other words, antigens are markers that identify specific pathogens. Each kind of pathogen has antigens that are unique to that particular type. For example, common cold viruses have antigens that are different from the antigens of all other pathogens—and from the antigens that normally live within your body.

Stop and Organize

Make notes in the second section of your Outline on page 36.

Antibodies

Once your immune system recognizes an antigen, it develops what are called antibodies that begin the fight against the pathogen. Antibodies are molecules produced by certain kinds of white blood cells. They can chemically neutralize poisons or destroy pathogens, including bacteria and viruses.

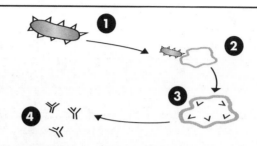

1. Bacteria invade the body.
2. Macrophages recognize bacteria that are foreign to the body and digest them.
3. Antigens from the destroyed bacteria move to the surfaces of the macrophages.
4. Antibodies that can destroy the invading bacteria are produced and released.

With the help of macrophages and antigens, the body is able to produce pathogen-destroying antibodies.

Stop and Organize

Make notes in the third section of your Outline on page 36.

C Plan

When you finish your preview, choose the strategy that you'll use to help you read and understand the science chapter.

• **An excellent strategy to use with science chapters is outlining.**

Create your Outline before you begin reading so that you can take notes on it as you go. Use chapter headings as the major headings in your Outline.

During Reading

D Read with a Purpose

Keep your Outline by your side as you read.

Directions: Now do a careful reading of the science chapter. Write your notes on the Outline on the following page.

Textbooks

Outline

I. Three types of immunity

  A.

    1.

    2.

    3.

  B.

    1.

    2.

    3.

  C.

    1.

    2.

    3.

II. Macrophages and antigens

  A.

  B.

  C.

III. Antibodies

  A.

  B.

  C.

Using the Strategy

Plan on doing at least two careful readings of every science chapter. On your second reading, add important details to your Outline.

Directions: Return to part I of your Outline and add specific facts and details.

Understanding How Science Texts Are Organized

Scientists often think in terms of cause and effect. You'll find that many science chapters are organized around this concept.

Directions: Think about what you learned in the immune system chapter. Then complete this organizer.

Cause-Effect Organizer

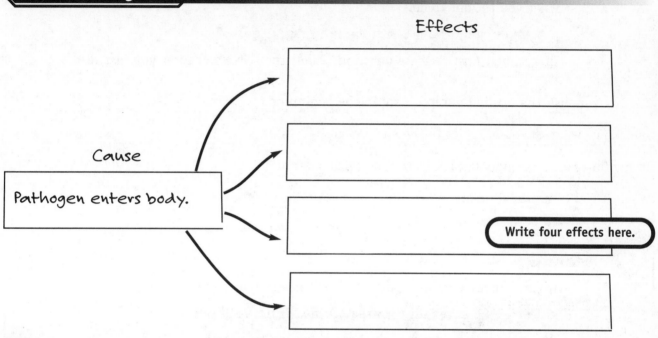

Effects

Cause

Pathogen enters body.

Write four effects here.

E Connect

The personal connections you make to a science reading can make the information easier to remember.

• **You can connect to a science chapter by recording what the subject reminds you of in your own life.**

Directions: Reread this paragraph from the science chapter. Then write what the information reminds you of from your own life.

Artificial active immunity occurs when a vaccination is given. When you receive a vaccine, dead or weakened pathogens are introduced into your body, usually in the form of an injection or serum (see Figure 11.9). In response, your body produces antibodies against these pathogens.

Textbooks

After Reading

When you finish reading a science chapter, review what you learned. Your Outline can help you stay focused on key facts and details.

F Pause and Reflect

Always return to your original reading purpose to see if you've accomplished what you set out to do.

• **Ask yourself, "Have I met my reading purpose?"**

Directions: Answer these questions about the science chapter you just read.

Did I accomplish the reading purpose I set in the beginning? ....

Do I know what the main topics in the chapter are? ....

In my Outline, can I support each main topic with subtopics? ....

Would I feel comfortable taking a test on this material now? ....

G Reread

If you haven't met your purpose, you'll need to do some rereading.

• **A powerful rereading strategy to use is note-taking.**

Directions: Make notes about key terms on these Study Cards.

Study Cards

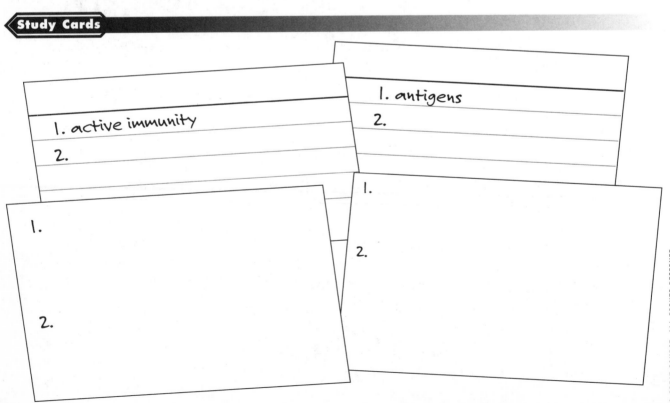

NAME _____

H Remember

It's important that you find a way to remember what you learn in any textbook. Chances are good that the information will appear on a future test.

• **Creating a practice test can help you remember the most important parts of a science chapter.**

Directions: Write three sample test questions. Then exchange questions with a partner and answer each other's questions.

Practice Test

Name of Partner

1. Question:

Answer:

2. Question:

Answer:

3. Question:

Answer:

Reading Math

The key to reading a math textbook is reading slowly, carefully, and actively. This will help you think critically and recall the necessary prior knowledge.

Before Reading

Use the reading process and the strategy of visualizing and thinking aloud to help you read and respond to the instructions, explanations, and examples found in a math textbook.

 ### A Set a Purpose

The easiest way to set your purpose for reading a math chapter is to turn the title of the chapter into a question.

• **To set your purpose, ask one or more questions about the title of the chapter.**

Directions: On the lines below, write your purpose questions for reading a math chapter called "Surface Area of a Prism."

Purpose question #1

....

....

Purpose question #2

....

....

Purpose question #3

....

....

NAME

 B **Preview**

Spend a few minutes previewing a math chapter before you begin reading. This will help you activate prior knowledge about the topic.

Directions: Preview the sample math chapter. Make notes on this K-W-L Chart.

K-W-L Chart

What I **K**now	What I **W**ant to Know	What I **L**earned

Chapter

7.7 Surface Area of a Prism

Goal
• Learn how to calculate the surface area of a prism.

Key Terms
prism
surface area

Goal Learn to calculate the surface area of a prism.

A **prism** is a three-dimensional figure that has two congruent and parallel faces that are polygons. The remaining faces are parallelograms. Prisms are named according to the shapes of their bases. For example:

✔ **Study Tip**
Recall what you know about calculating lateral area. Reread pages 100–104 for help.

A triangular prism   A hexagonal prism

The surface area of a prism is the sum of all the areas of its faces, including the bases. To find the **surface area** (SA), find the area of both bases (2B), and add the sum of the areas of the lateral faces (the lateral area, LA):

SA = (2B + LA)

Real-life connection:

Example Find the surface area of this triangular prism.

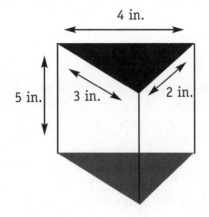

4 in.

5 in.   3 in.   2 in.

Formulas

To find the lateral area of a triangle, use this formula:

A = 1/2 x bh

To find the lateral area of a rectangle, use this formula:

A = lw

Textbooks

Solution

Area of 2 triangular faces = 2 X 1/2 X 2 X 3 = 6 sq. in.

Area of 2-by-5 rectangular face = 2 X 5 = 10 sq. in.

Area of 3-by-5 rectangular face = 3 X 5 = 15 sq. in.

Area of 4-by-5 rectangular face = 4 X 5 = 20 sq. in.

Surface area = 6 + 10 + 15 + 20 = 51 sq. in.

Double-check ✔✔

Apply What You've Learned

Calculate the surface area of this prism.

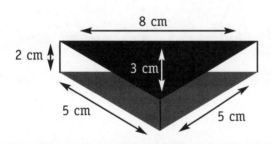

8 cm

2 cm   3 cm

5 cm   5 cm

Plan

The best strategy to use with a math textbook is visualizing and thinking aloud.

• **Visualizing and thinking aloud with math means that you make a drawing or talk yourself through the steps in a process.**

During Reading

D Read with a Purpose

Remember that your purpose is to learn the skills taught in the chapter.

Directions: Now do a careful reading of the sample math chapter on calculating the surface area of a prism. Write your thoughts on the sticky notes.

Using the Strategy

Thinking aloud is using your own words to explain what you must do to solve the problem.

Directions: Read this practice problem from the same math chapter. Write a Think Aloud that tells how you would solve it.

Sample Problem

Calculate the surface area of this prism.

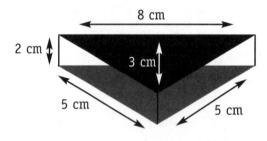

Think Aloud

....

....

....

....

....

....

....

Understanding How Math Textbooks Are Organized

Most math chapters contain some type of study guide that lists key objectives and the terms you need to know. For example:

Goal	Key Terms
• Learn how to calculate the surface area of a prism.	prism surface area

Directions: Answer these questions using the notes you made while reading the sample math chapter.

What is a prism?

_____

_____

What is the surface area of a prism?

_____

What formula do you use to calculate surface area?

_____

E **Connect**

Math will feel more relevant to your life if you turn abstract problems into real-life ones.

• **Connecting a math problem to the real world can make the problem easier to solve.**

Directions: Review the chart at the top of page 109 of the *Reader's Handbook.* Then write a real-life problem for the abstract problem shown in the chart below.

◄ Real-life Problem

Abstract Problem	Real-life Problem
10" 3" 3"	

After Reading

After you finish a math chapter, think carefully about what you learned.

F Pause and Reflect

Return to the purpose you set before reading the chapter and ask yourself, "Did I learn what this chapter was trying to teach me?"

- **After you finish a math chapter, ask yourself, "How well did I meet my purpose?"**

<u>Directions:</u> Answer these questions about the prism surface area chapter.

Looking Back

Do I understand the key terms?
Do I know how to calculate the surface area of a prism?
Are the examples clear to me?
Can I solve one or more surface area problems on my own?
Would I do well on a test that covered this material?

G Reread

Think about the information you learned from the chapter. If you don't understand it completely, you need to do some rereading.

- **Use the rereading strategy of note-taking to help you process and remember information in the chapter.**

<u>Directions:</u> Read the concepts in the left-hand column. Write your own example of the concept in the right-hand column.

Key Word Notes

Key Words and Concepts	Examples
prism	
surface area	
calculating surface area	

NAME ....

FOR USE WITH PAGES 100–111

 ## Remember

Remember that math concepts build on each other, like blocks in a pyramid. Don't move on to a new chapter until you're sure you understand the chapter you just read.

• **Creating a practice test can serve as an important review of the material you just read.**

Directions: Write a practice test on calculating the surface area of a prism. Then write an answer key.

▶ **Practice Test**

◀ **Answer Key** ▶

Textbooks

Focus on Foreign Language

The reading process works even with foreign language textbooks. Follow these steps to get more out of your study of a foreign language.

Step 1: Read the text.

Always begin with an active reading. Make notes as you go.

Directions: Read the following page from a Spanish textbook. Then complete the sticky note.

Los Verbos *Ser* y *Estar*

➤➤ The verbs *ser* and *estar* both mean "to be," but only *ser* is used to express origin, nationality, relationships of equivalence, time, possession, and what something is made of:

Soy de Barcelona.
I am from Barcelona.

Luz es mi amiga.
Luz is my friend.

Estas manzanas son de Cristina.
These are Christine's apples.

El pastel es de harina.
The cake is made of flour.

➤➤ *Estar* refers to location:

Tía Lila está en su cocina.
Aunt Lila is in her kitchen.

La biblioteca está cerca de la escuela.
The library is near the school.

Ejercicios

Completa las frases usando la forma correcta de *ser* or *estar*:

Eduardo	contento.
Las galletas	buenas.
El bolso	de cuero.
Mis abuelos	ingleses.

Objectives

Learn the correct uses for the verbs *ser* and *estar*.

NOTA

Both *ser* and *estar* are used with adjectives, but each is used for a slightly different purpose. *Ser* is used with an adjective that expresses a characteristic of a person or thing:

Tino es simpático.
(Tino is nice.)

Estar is used with adjectives to express a quality that is not always applicable:

Tino está cansado.
(Tino is tired.)

What is the textbook page about?

Step 2: Organize what you've learned.

Next, make an organizer that explores what you learned. This will help you process and remember the information.

Directions: Record your notes from the reading in the following diagram.

> **Venn Diagram**

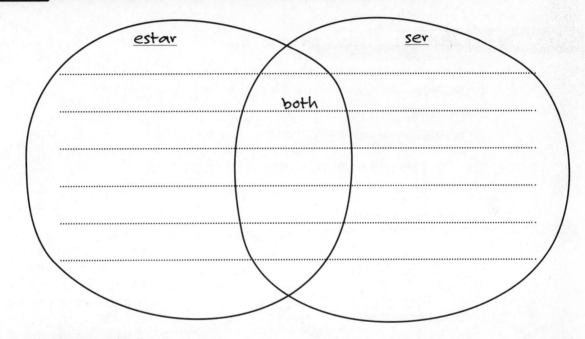

Step 3: Commit what you've learned to memory.

Memorizing is an important part of learning a foreign language. Creating a study test can help.

Directions: Read the review tips on page 117 of the *Reader's Handbook*. Then write three test questions for the Spanish page you read.

> **Sample Test**

....

....

....

....

....

....

Focus on Science Concepts

Most science textbooks include concepts and processes that you need to study and memorize. Following these steps can help.

Step 1: Learn key terms.

A science concept is a process, or series of steps, that explains a phenomenon. To understand a science concept, you must first familiarize yourself with its terminology.

Directions: Look at the inflammatory response diagram below. It shows how your body responds to an injury. Write key words in the word bank on the next page. Then use a dictionary to define each term.

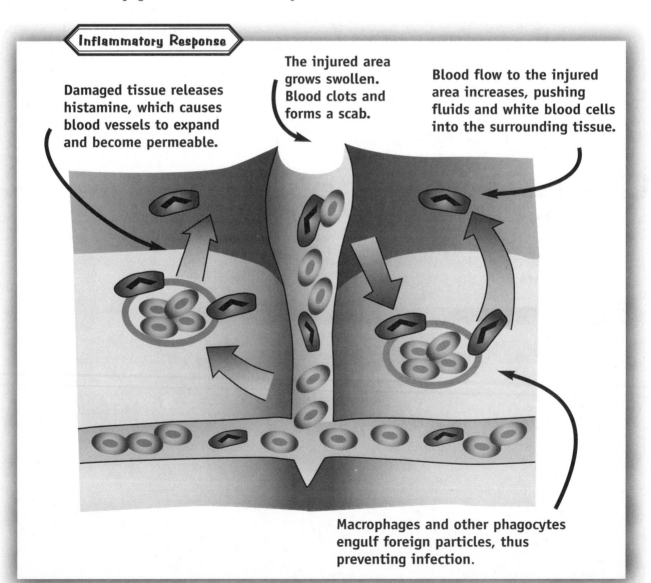

Inflammatory Response

Damaged tissue releases histamine, which causes blood vessels to expand and become permeable.

The injured area grows swollen. Blood clots and forms a scab.

Blood flow to the injured area increases, pushing fluids and white blood cells into the surrounding tissue.

Macrophages and other phagocytes engulf foreign particles, thus preventing infection.

Directions: Write the steps of the inflammatory response here. Use key terms from your word bank.

◀ **Word Bank** ▶

Word	Definition
histamine	
white blood cells	
permeable	
macrophages	
phagocytes	

Step 2: Track steps in the process.

Next, figure out how the process works, step by step.

Directions: Write the steps of inflammatory response in the chart on the next page. Use key terms from your word bank.

Textbooks

Flow Chart

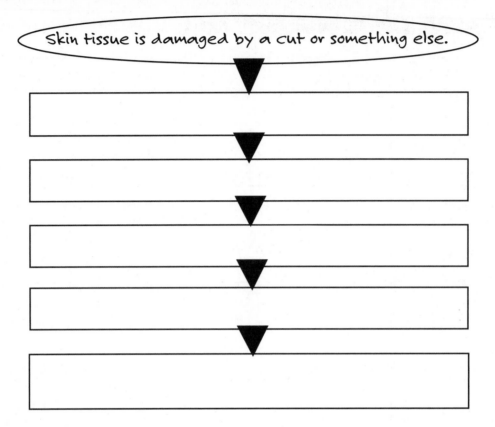

Skin tissue is damaged by a cut or something else.

Step 3: Retell the process.

Finish by retelling the process to a friend. The act of retelling makes it easier for you to retain what you've learned.

Directions: Retell the steps of the inflammatory response on the lines below. Refer to your notes as needed.

Retelling

....

....

....

....

....

....

NAME ....

FOR USE WITH PAGES 125–128

Focus on Study Questions

It's important that you read all test and study questions carefully, even if you're certain you know the answer. Follow this four-step plan.

Step 1: Read the question twice.

Begin by reading the question at least twice. Note any key words.

Directions: Read this sample question. Highlight the words and phrases that you think are important.

Sample Question

In 1517, a German clergyman named Martin Luther started a religious revolt, or protest, against the church. Discuss three causes for this revolt, which came to be called the "Protestant Reformation."

Step 2: Choose a strategy.

In most cases, the best strategy to use with study or test questions is visualizing and thinking aloud. See page 126 in the *Reader's Handbook* if you need to review how to use this strategy.

Directions: On the lines below, explain what you need to do to answer the sample question. Then explain how the strategy of thinking aloud can help.

....

....

....

....

....

....

....

Textbooks

Step 3: Answer the question.

Next, use the strategy to answer the question.

Directions: Write a Think Aloud that tells how you would answer the sample question.

◀ **Think Aloud**

....

....

....

....

....

....

....

....

....

....

....

....

....

....

Step 4: Check your answer.

The last step is to check your work. Reread the question and your answer. Ask yourself, "Is my answer reasonable?"

Directions: Reread your Think Aloud. Then exchange books with a partner. Read your partner's writing and make comments in the margin.

Focus on Word Problems

Math word problems only seem tricky. The key to solving them is reading carefully, visualizing, and thinking aloud.

Step 1: Read the problem.

Always read the problem more than once, until you understand it completely. Highlight key words and make notes.

Directions: Read this sample word problem. Highlight key words and list what you learned on the sticky note.

Sample Problem

Jasel sets his computer to do an auto-save every 4 minutes. How many times does the computer save his work in a 3-hour period?

The topic is:

The given is:

I need to find:

Step 2: Choose a strategy.

Use the strategy of visualizing and thinking aloud with word problems.

Directions: Make a sketch that shows the auto-save problem.

Visualizing

Step 3: Solve.

Now solve the problem.

Directions: Write a numerical expression for the auto-save problem. Then solve it.

....
....
....
....
....
....
....

Step 4: Check.

Your last step is to check your work and see if your answer makes sense.

Directions: Write a Think Aloud that shows how you solved the auto-save problem.

◀ **Think Aloud**

....
....
....
....
....
....
....
....
....

Reading a Personal Essay

Most personal essays are informal, even conversational, in tone. But don't be misled. The author has an important message, and it's your job to find it.

Before Reading

On the pages that follow, you'll be asked to read and respond to a personal essay. Use the reading process and the strategy of outlining to help.

A Set a Purpose

When reading and analyzing a personal essay, your primary purpose is to find the subject and main idea. It is also important to decide how you feel about the essayist's main idea.

• **To set your purpose, ask questions about the essay's subject and main idea.**

Directions: Write three purpose questions for the essay "Pleasure Boat Studio." Then make a prediction about the essay.

Purpose question 1:

Purpose question 2:

Purpose question 3:

My prediction:

B Preview

Always preview an essay before you begin reading. Pay careful attention to the items on this checklist.

Preview Checklist

☐ the title and author

☐ the first and last paragraphs

☐ any repeated words

Nonfiction

Directions: Preview "Pleasure Boat Studio." Write your preview notes on this Web.

Web

Author's name:
....
....

Essay subject:
....
....
....
....

Repeated words:
....
....
....

Background information:
....
....
....
....
....
....
....
....
....
....
....

First paragraph details:
....
....
....
....
....
....
....
....
....
....

"Pleasure Boat Studio"

Last paragraph details:
....
....
....
....

NAME

from "Pleasure Boat Studio" by Ou-Yang Hsiu

Ou-Yang Hsiu (1007–1072) was a poet and essayist of the Sung dynasty in China. He is considered one of the eight "masters" of Chinese classical prose and is remembered in particular for his powers of description. "Pleasure Boat Studio" is a descriptive and reflective essay. In it, the author describes his studio, reflects upon the name he gave it and what it means to him, and ends with a short explanation of why he wrote the essay. The device of ending with a few words about the essay itself was common in ancient Chinese writings.

Three months after I came to Hua I converted the rooms of the eastern wing of the government offices into a place for me to spend my leisure time. I named it "Pleasure Boat Studio." The studio is one room across and seven rooms long (the rooms being connected with doorways), and so to walk into my studio is just like walking into a boat. First, in a corner of the warm room I made a hole in the roof to let in light. Then on either side of the bright and open unwalled rooms I installed railings to sit on or lean against. Anyone who relaxes in my studio will find that it is just like relaxing on a boat. The craggy stone mounds and the flowering plants and trees that I arranged just beyond the eaves on both sides make it seem all the more that one is drifting down the middle of a river, with the mountains on the right facing forests on the left, all very attractive. This, then, is why I named my studio after a boat.

Stop and Organize

Make some notes in the Introduction section of the Outline on page 61.

In "Judgment," of the *Book of Changes*, whenever one encounters dangerous circumstances, the advice is always: "Cross the River." One can see from this that the real purpose of boats is to deliver people from danger rather than to provide comfort. But now I have converted part of the government offices into a studio for relaxation and have named it after a boat—was that not a perverse thing to do? Furthermore, I myself was once banished to the rivers and lakes because of my crimes. I sailed down the Pien River, crossed the Huai, and floated along the mighty Yangtze as far as Pa Gorges. Then I turned and went up the Han-mien River. In all, I must have covered several thousand miles on water. During those wearisome travels, when I was unlucky enough to encounter sudden storms or rough waters, many times I cried aloud to the gods to spare my brief life. In one such moment, as I looked ahead and behind, I noticed that the only other people out in boats were all either merchants or government officials. I sighed as I thought to myself: except for men who are anxious for profit and those who have no choice, who would be caught out here?

from "Pleasure Boat Studio" by Ou-Yang Hsiu, continued

By Heaven's grace, I came through all such crises alive. Moreover, today my former misdeeds have been forgiven and I have been reinstated at Court. This is why I have now come to this prefecture where I eat my fill on public food and live comfortably in government quarters. As I think back on all the mountains I passed through and all the dangers my boat was exposed to, when dragons and water-serpents surfaced around me and high waves broke and surged on all sides, it is hardly surprising that I am sometimes frightened from my sleep by nightmares. And yet now I disregard all the dangers I faced and name my studio after a boat. Can it be that I am fond of life afloat after all?

I have heard of men of antiquity who fled from the world to distant rivers and lakes and refused to their dying day to return. They must have found some source of pleasure there. If one is not anxious for profit, even at the risk of danger, or is not convicted of a crime and forced to embark; rather, if one has a favorable breeze and gentle seas and is able to rest comfortably on a pillow and mat, sailing several hundred miles in a single day, then is boat travel not enjoyable? Of course, I have no time for such diversions. But since "pleasure boat" is the designation of boats used for such pastimes, I have now adopted it as the name of my studio. Is there anything wrong with that?

Stop and Organize
Make some more notes in the Body section of the Outline on page 61.

My friend, Ts'ai Chün-mo (Ts'ai Hsiang) excels at large style calligraphy. His writing is quite unusual and imposing. I have decided to ask him to write out my studio's name in large characters, which I will display on a pillar. I feared, however, that some people might not understand why I chose the name I did, and so I wrote out this explanation and inscribed it on the wall.

Written on the twelfth day of the twelfth month in the Jen-wu year
(January 25, 1043).

Stop and Organize
Make some notes in the Conclusion section of the Outline on page 61.

 **Plan**

Next, choose a strategy that can help you meet your purpose. Many readers find that the strategy of outlining can help them get more from an essay.

• **Outlining can help you sort important from unimportant details in the essay.**

During Reading

Mentally dividing the essay into three parts (Introduction, Body, and Conclusion) can make the author's message easier to find.

D **Read with a Purpose**

Keep your purpose questions in mind as you read. Remember that you are looking for the subject and main idea of the essay.

Directions: Now do a careful reading of "Pleasure Boat Studio." Write your notes on this Outline.

Outline

I. Introduction

A. Detail:

B. Detail:

C. Detail:

II. Body

A. Detail:

B. Detail:

C. Detail:

III. Conclusion

A. Detail:

B. Detail:

C. Detail:

Nonfiction

Using the Strategy

Use your Outline notes to find the main idea of an essay. Follow this formula:

subject + how the author feels about the subject = the main point

Directions: Find the main idea of "Pleasure Boat Studio."

.... + ...

subject   how the author feels

= ....

....

main point

Understanding How Essays Are Organized

Most personal essays are organized in a funnel pattern.

• In a funnel pattern, the writer has building blocks for the main idea.

Directions: Reread the discussion on how personal essays are organized on page 163 of the *Reader's Handbook*. Then complete this organizer.

Editorial Structure

Name the topic here. ....

List details that relate to the topic here. ....

....

....

....

Write a key detail from the conclusion here. ....

....

....

Write the essayist's main idea here. ....

....

....

 **Connect**

One of the ways you can sharpen your reading skills is by making connections to a text. An obvious way to connect to an essay is to ask yourself, "What do I think about the essayist's ideas?"

- **Connect to an essay by recording your thoughts and feelings about the main idea.**

<u>Directions:</u> Read these sentences from the essay. Write your reaction to it on the sticky note.

> My friend, Ts'ai Chün-mo (Ts'ai Hsiang) excels at large style calligraphy. His writing is quite unusual and imposing. I have decided to ask him to write out my studio's name in large characters, which I will display on a pillar. I feared, however, that some people might not understand why I chose the name I did, and so I wrote out this explanation and inscribed it on the wall.

Nonfiction

After Reading

When you finish reading, take a moment or two to think about what the author has said.

 Pause and Reflect

Ask yourself questions about the essay and your purpose for reading.

- **After you finish an essay, ask yourself, "How well did I meet my purpose?"**

<u>Directions:</u> Answer these questions about Ou-Yang Hsiu's essay.

Looking Back

What is the subject of the essay?

....

What does the author say about the subject?

....

....

....

....

Do you feel you've met your reading purpose?

....

....

Reread

The strategy of questioning the author can help you if you're not sure you understand a point made in the essay.

• **A powerful rereading strategy to use with personal essays is questioning the author.**

Directions: Write two questions that you would like to ask Ou-Yang Hsiu. Then write the answers you think he might have given.

Questioning the Author

Question 1: ....
....

Ou-Yang Hsiu's answer: ....

....

....

Question 2: ....
....

Ou-Yang Hsiu's answer: ....

....

....

 Remember

Always find a way to remember what you've read.

• **Creating a Main Idea Organizer can help you retain the most important facts and details from a personal essay.**

Directions: Complete this organizer using notes from your reading.

Main Idea Organizer

Topic:		
Main Idea:		
Detail 1	**Detail 2**	**Detail 3**

Reading an

Editorials are a type of persuasive writing. In most editorials, the writer advances an opinion or furthers an argument about an important issue of the day. Your job is to understand and evaluate the assertions the writer makes.

Before Reading

Practice reading and responding to an editorial here. Use the strategy of questioning the author to help you read an editorial that was first published in *The Crisis*, the magazine of the National Association for the Advancement of Colored People (NAACP).

A Set a Purpose

Your purpose for reading an editorial involves identifying the author's viewpoint, evaluating how persuasively the point is made, and deciding how you feel about it.

- **To set your purpose, ask questions about the viewpoint and the support presented.**

Directions: Write your purpose questions for reading the editorial "Let Us Reason Together" on the lines below.

Purpose question #1 ....

Purpose question #2 ....

Purpose question #3 ....

B Preview

Preview the editorial to get a sense of the subject. Watch for items on this checklist:

Preview Checklist

☐ where the editorial was published

☐ the headline and date

☐ any repeated words

☐ the first and last paragraphs

Nonfiction

Directions: Preview "Let Us Reason Together." Write your preview notes in the following chart.

Preview Chart

Items Previewed	My Notes
the headline	
the author	
the date	
the first paragraph	
the last paragraph	
repeated words and phrases	

After World War I, there was an event in America that came to be called "The Great Migration." During this time, tens of thousands of African Americans migrated from their homes in the South to the major cities of the North. They came in search of better jobs, higher wages, and the social equality that they had been long denied in the South. White American city-dwellers, who were afraid for their jobs, greeted the blacks with clubs and stones, rather than open arms. A series of bloody race riots occurred. W. E. B. DuBois, who at the time was editor of the influential African American magazine The Crisis, *wrote this editorial in the days following the Chicago race riots of 1919.*

Volume 18: Issue 231   **THE CRISIS**   September 19, 1919

LET US REASON TOGETHER

by W. E. B. DuBois

Brothers, we are on the Great Deep. We have cast off on the vast voyage which will lead to Freedom or Death.

For three centuries we have suffered and cowered. No race ever gave Passive Resistance and Submission to Evil a longer, more piteous trial. Today we raise the terrible weapon of Self-Defense. When the murderer comes, he shall no longer strike us in the back. When the

"Let Us Reason Together," by W. E. B. DuBois, continued

armed lynchers gather, we too must gather armed. When the mob moves, we propose to meet it with bricks and clubs and guns.

Stop and Organize
Why does DuBois begin by talking about what has happened in the past? Make notes on your Double-entry Journal on page 68.

But we must tread here with solemn caution. We must never let justifiable self-defense against individuals become blind and lawless offense against all white folk. We must not seek reform by violence. We must not seek Vengeance. "Vengeance is Mine," saith the Lord; or to put it otherwise, only Infinite Justice and Knowledge can assign blame in this poor world, and we ourselves are sinful men, struggling desperately with our own crime and ignorance. We must defend ourselves, our homes, our wives and children against the lawless without stint or hesitation: but we must carefully and scrupulously avoid on our own part bitter and unjustifiable aggression against anybody.

This line is difficult to draw. In the South the Police and Public Opinion back the mob and the least resistance on the part of the innocent black victim is nearly always construed as a lawless attack on society and government. In the North the Police and the Public will dodge and falter, but in the end they will back the Right when the Truth is made clear to them.

But whether the line between just resistance and angry retaliation is hard or easy, we must draw it carefully, not in wild resentment, but in grim and sober consideration: and then in back of the impregnable fortress of the Divine Right of Self-Defense, which is sanctioned by every law of God and man, in every land, civilized and uncivilized, we must take our unfaltering stand.

Stop and Organize
What point is DuBois making about self-defense here? Make notes on your Double-entry Journal on page 68.

Honor, endless and undying Honor, to every man, black or white, who in Houston, East St. Louis, Washington, and Chicago gave his life for Civilization and Order.

If the United States is to be a Land of Law, we would live humbly and peaceably in it—working, singing, learning, and dreaming to make it and ourselves nobler and better: if it is to be a Land of Mobs and Lynchers, we might as well die today as tomorrow.

> *"And how can man die better*
> *Than facing fearful odds*
> *For the ashes of his fathers*
> *And the temples of his gods?"*

Stop and Organize
What action are readers supposed to take or how are readers supposed to feel as a result of this editorial? Make notes on your Double-entry Journal on page 68.

Nonfiction

C Plan

At the planning stage, choose a strategy that can help you figure out the writer's viewpoint and supporting information.

- **Use the strategy of questioning the author to help you find the writer's assertions.**

During Reading

D Read with a Purpose

Remember your purpose questions. In addition to finding the viewpoint, you need to think about how you will evaluate the argument as a whole.

Directions: Do a careful reading of the editorial. Ask questions of the author. Make notes on this Double-entry Journal.

Double-entry Journal

Questions	My Thoughts
Why does DuBois begin by talking about what has happened in the past?	
What point is DuBois making about self-defense here?	
What action are readers supposed to take or how are they supposed to feel as a result of this editorial?	

Using the Strategy

After you ask and answer questions of the author, use a Critical Reading Chart to evaluate the information the author has presented.

Directions: Record your answers to these critical reading questions.

Critical Reading Chart

Questions	My Thoughts
1. What topic is the writer discussing?	
2. How does the writer feel about the topic?	
3. What are the writer's assertions?	
4. How does the writer support the assertions?	
5. What do I think about this topic?	
6. How do my thoughts compare with those of the writer?	

Nonfiction

Understanding How Editorials Are Organized

Generally editorials have three parts: assertion, support, and recommendation. Reread the section about the three parts of an editorial on page 175 of the *Reader's Handbook* as a review.

- **Most editorials contain three parts: an assertion, support for the assertion, and a recommendation.**

Directions: Record the writer's assertions, support, and recommendation in "Let Us Reason Together" on this organizer.

Parts of an Editorial

Assertion

Supporting detail

▼

Assertion

Supporting detail

▼

Recommendation

E Connect

Connecting to an editorial means considering how the writing makes you feel.

- **Connect to an editorial by recording your thoughts and feelings.**

Directions: Reread the final section of the editorial. Then write your thoughts on the sticky note.

If the United States is to be a Land of Law, we would live humbly and peaceably in it—working, singing, learning, and dreaming to make it and ourselves nobler and better: if it is to be a Land of Mobs and Lynchers, we might as well die today as tomorrow.

"And how can man die better
Than facing fearful odds
For the ashes of his fathers
And the temples of his gods?"

Here is how I feel about the writer's argument:

....

....

....

....

After Reading

Reflecting on what you've read in an editorial can help you decide whether or not you agree with the writer's assertion.

F Pause and Reflect

When you pause and reflect, ask yourself questions about the editorial and your purpose for reading.

• **After you finish an essay, ask yourself, "How well did I meet my purpose?"**

Directions: Answer these questions about DuBois's editorial.

Questions

Do you understand DuBois's assertions?

_____

Why did he use that headline for his editorial?

_____

Can you explain how he supports the assertions?

_____

_____

Do you know how you feel about his argument?

_____

_____

Reread

How can you get the most out of your second reading of an editorial? The reading strategy of synthesizing will help.

• **Synthesizing means examining bits of information from a piece of writing and then putting them together to see what they mean.**

Directions: Complete the following Synthesizing Chart. Use the notes you made while reading DuBois's editorial.

Synthesizing Chart

Topic	My Thoughts
What are the author's assertions?	
Supporting detail #1	
Supporting detail #2	

NAME ....

H Remember

Good readers remember what they've read. Writing a letter to the editor can help.

• **Writing a letter can help you remember the most important points in an editorial.**

Directions: Write a brief letter in which you respond to the points DuBois makes in his editorial. Express your opinion about his assertion and discuss whether the argument is effective.

Letter

....
....
....
....
....
....
....
....
....

NAME ....

FOR USE WITH PAGES 181–192

Reading a News Story

You read a newspaper to find out what's happening in your neighborhood and in the world. Good news stories provide the facts you need and compel you to read to the very end.

Before Reading

Here you'll use the reading process to help you read and understand a news story that was published in 1937.

 A ### Set a Purpose

When you read a news story, your primary purpose is to answer these six questions: *who, what, where, when, why,* and *how.*

• **To set your purpose, ask six questions about the news story.**

Directions: Write your purpose questions for reading the news story "Two Inmates Vanish from Alcatraz" on the lines below.

Setting a Purpose

	My Purpose Questions
Who?	
What?	
Where?	
When?	
Why?	
How?	

Preview

Find out as much as you can about the topic of the story during your preview. Pay attention to items on this organizer.

Directions: Read the lead of the Alcatraz news story. Make notes on this 5 W's and H Organizer.

5 W's and H Organizer

Subject:

Who	What	Where	When	Why	How

Nonfiction

The San Francisco Crier

Two Inmates Vanish from Alcatraz

ALCATRAZ ISLAND, DECEMBER 17—
Yesterday afternoon, two inmates of the U.S. Penitentiary at Alcatraz Island squeezed through a broken prison window and disappeared into the dense fog blanketing the island. The escapees were Alcatraz inmate #58-AZ, Theodore Cole, and inmate #260-AZ, Ralph Roe. Despite a massive manhunt that began within an hour of the inmates' escape, not a trace of either man has been found.

The Search Begins

At approximately 1:30 P.M. yesterday, a prison guard sounded the alarm indicating a possible prison break. The guard notified the watchtowers that Roe and Cole were unaccounted for, and that they had last been seen in the tire recycling area of the prison's work building. Both were present at the 12:30 P.M. count, but were noticeably absent from the 1:30 count.

Shortly after the alarm went out, another guard in the work building discovered a window from which two iron bars had been cut through and three heavy panes of glass had been smashed. Prison authorities assume that Cole and Roe squeezed through the window and then made their way to the high mesh wire fence that surrounds the perimeter of the work building. The thick fog likely prevented them from being seen.

Escapees Used Prison's Own Tools to Smash Gate

Clearly the fog was a help to the two men. But it's possible that they had additional help in the form of a heavy, long-handled wrench that they might have used to break one of the padlocks on the perimeter fence. An Alcatraz guard, who wishes to remain anonymous, reports that a Stillson wrench, similar to the type used in the tire recycling shop, was found abandoned near a gate of the perimeter fence.

Prison officials surmise that from the fence, Cole and Roe made their way down a steep ledge and then made a break for the shoreline. Although no trace of flotation devices has been found, many assume that the two escapees used oil drums or even old tires to help them swim to freedom.

A Frantic Warden Sends for Help as the Hours Tick By

As soon as the escape alarm went out, Prison Warden James A. Johnson rushed to one of the many guard towers on the island and began scanning the choppy waters surrounding Alcatraz Island. "I kept going from tower to tower using the binoculars," Warden Johnson reported, "but all I could see was driftwood coming down from the

> **"Two Inmates Vanish from Alcatraz,"** continued

rivers, churning up and down, swirling round and round, and being carried to the ocean in a swift, rushing, outgoing tide."

Stop and Record

What facts does the reporter give? What opinions? Record them on your Critical Reading Chart on page 79.

Assuming the men had drowned, but unwilling to take any chances, the warden called for assistance. By 2:30 P.M., a prison boat was circling the spot where the two men were believed to have escaped, while five United States Coast Guard vessels patrolled the waters surrounding Alcatraz.

In addition, guards from Alcatraz were immediately dispatched to the San Francisco, Marin County, and East Bay shores. Search parties were formed with the help of local police officers. Officials sent out an all-points bulletin and alerted the California Highway Patrol to keep a close watch on all northbound roads.

Two Hardened Criminals Plan Their Escape

Prison officials have been maintaining a strict policy of "no comment" when asked for information about Cole and Roe's background. But some Alcatraz guards have been much more forthcoming and have provided many details about the two escaped convicts.

The *San Francisco Crier* has learned that Roe and Cole were both hardened criminals who have spent much of their lives behind bars. Ralph Roe, who is thought to be the mastermind behind the escape plan, was serving time at Alcatraz for bank robbery and kidnapping. "He was doing ninety-nine years and he was doing them hard," a loose-lipped Alcatraz guard reported.

The same might be said for Roe's partner in the escape, Theodore Cole. Like Roe, Cole has spent most of his life in one prison or another. Most recently, he was tried, convicted, and sentenced to fifty years for the kidnapping of a farmer at gunpoint.

Due to the serious nature of their crimes, Roe and Cole were both sent to Alcatraz, a prison with a reputation of "maximum security and minimum privilege." Despite Alcatraz's high guard-to-prisoner ratio, Roe and Cole most likely began planning their escape almost as soon as they arrived at the "Rock," which is the nickname given to the prison at Alcatraz Island.

Stop and Record

How do you think the reporter feels about Roe and Cole? Make notes on your Critical Reading Chart on page 79.

Escape from Alcatraz Thought "Impossible"

Early this morning, prison officials acknowledged that Roe and Cole's escape gave them a shock because they thought that escape from Alcatraz was impossible. "I just can't believe it," a

Nonfiction

"Two Inmates Vanish from Alcatraz," continued

guard declared. "I mean, this place is secure. We have tool-proof bars on every cell and metal detectors everywhere."

An even more effective deterrent to escape is the fact that the prison sits at the highest point on Alcatraz Island, a barren, wind-tossed piece of land in the middle of the San Francisco Bay. Alcatraz officials and others assumed that if the unthinkable happened and a prisoner managed to escape the prison itself, he would surely drown before reaching the mainland, which is well over a mile away.

The Hunt Continues

The fact remains, however, that despite the sophisticated security at Alcatraz, Roe and Cole *did* manage to escape without a trace. Many officials, including Warden Johnson, maintain that the escapees pose no threat to the

general public, however, because they never made it to the San Francisco shoreline. "I believe they drowned and their bodies were swept out toward the Golden Gate," Johnson told the press. "The tide would have carried them right out the gate and into the sea."

Nevertheless, rumors have been circulating that the FBI is about to join the hunt, and that they will be looking for a pair of live criminals rather than two dead bodies. As always, the *San Francisco Crier* will keep you informed of any and all new developments.

Stop and Record

Are the reporter's sources authoritative and reliable? Make notes on your Critical Reading Chart on page 79.

Plan

Next, form a plan that can help you meet your purpose for reading the news story.

> **• The strategy of reading critically works well with newspaper articles.**

Reading critically means examining the facts presented and deciding how reliable they are. For more information on the strategy, see your *Reader's Handbook,* pages 185–186.

During Reading

D Read with a Purpose

Once you have your plan in place, you can begin reading the article.

Directions: Read "Two Inmates Vanish from Alcatraz." Write your During Reading notes on this Critical Reading Chart.

Critical Reading Chart

My Questions	My Answers
What are the facts, and what are the opinions?	
What is the reporter's main idea?	
Are the sources authoritative and reliable?	
What's the other side of the story?	

Nonfiction

Using the Strategy

Reading critically means sifting through and interpreting the facts presented.

Directions: Complete this Outline using information from the news story you just read. Refer to your During Reading notes.

Outline

I. Information about the escape

A.

B.

C.

II. Information about the manhunt

A.

B.

C.

III. Reactions from officials and others

A.

B.

C.

Understanding How News Stories Are Organized

The standard lead of a news story contains answers to some or all of the six questions: *who, what, where, when, why,* and *how.*

• **Look for key facts about the subject in the lead of the story.**

Directions: Reread the Alcatraz article lead. Highlight clues about *who, what,* and *where.* Circle clues about *when* and *how.*

ALCATRAZ ISLAND, DECEMBER 17 — Yesterday afternoon, two inmates of the U.S. Penitentiary at Alcatraz Island squeezed through a broken prison window and disappeared into the dense fog blanketing the island. The escapees were Alcatraz inmate #58-AZ, Theodore Cole, and inmate #260-AZ, Ralph Roe. Despite a massive manhunt that began within an hour of the inmates' escape, not a trace of either man has been found.

E Connect

Think about how the information in a news story applies to you. This can make the story more interesting and meaningful.

- **To connect to a news story, ask yourself, "How does this apply to me?" or "What else do I know about this subject?"**

Directions: Answer these questions about the Alcatraz escape article.

How did you feel as you were reading the article?

What else do you know about Alcatraz?

After Reading

Good readers understand, respond to, and remember a news story's key facts.

F Pause and Reflect

Take a moment to reflect on what you've learned from the news story.

- **Ask yourself, "Can I answer *who, what, where, when, why,* and *how?*"**

Directions: Answer these questions about the Alcatraz escape story.
Then explain your answers.

Questions

Decide	Yes	No
I can answer who, what, where, when, and why questions.		
I know which details are facts and which are opinions.		
I understand the article's main idea.		
I can find three or more details used to support the main idea.		

My explanation:

How I'll find answers to my questions:

Reread

If you haven't met your reading purpose, you need to return to the text.
Either reread the whole story, or skim for key facts and carefully reread these.

• **A powerful rereading strategy to use with a news story is summarizing.**

<u>Directions:</u> Write a paragraph-by-paragraph summary of the Alcatraz
escape story. Write one brief sentence for each paragraph.

Paragraph-by-Paragraph Notes

Paragraph #	Most Important Fact
1	
2	
3	
4	
5	
6	
7	
8	
9	
10	
11	
12	
13	
14	
15	
16	

Remember

Good readers figure out a way to remember what they've read.

• **Creating a graphic organizer will help you remember facts and details from the news story.**

Directions: Write the main idea of the Alcatraz escape story. Then write three details that support the main idea. Use direct quotations from the text where possible.

Main Idea Organizer

Subject		
Main Idea		
Detail 1	**Detail 2**	**Detail 3**
Related Quotation:	**Related Quotation:**	**Related Quotation:**

Nonfiction

Reading a Biography

A biographer usually has two goals in mind when writing: to tell an interesting story about the events in a person's life and to create a portrait or impression of the person.

Before Reading

Here you'll use the reading process and the strategy of searching for cause and effect to help you read and respond to a biography of a Sioux Indian chief named Spotted Tail.

 A ## Set a Purpose

Your purpose for reading a biography is to learn about the subject's life. In addition, you'll read to form an impression of the subject.

• **To set your purpose, ask questions about the biographical subject.**

<u>Directions:</u> Write your purpose for reading a biography about Chief Spotted Tail here. Then explain what you already know about the Sioux Indians.

My purpose: ....

Here's what I already know about the Sioux: ....

....

....

....

 B ## Preview

A great way to preview a biography is to examine the front and back covers. Look for important information about the biographical subject.

<u>Directions:</u> Preview *Spotted Tail*. Complete the sticky notes as you preview.

Back Cover

Meet Spotted Tail— an admired peacemaker and terrifying warrior. . .

The mid-1800s was a time of transition for the Sioux and other Plains Indian nations. Their chiefs had signed land treaties granting whites parcels of land in the Great Plains. Before the ink on the treaties was dry, however, white settlers were demanding more and more Indian territory for their own.

A few Sioux leaders argued it was best to keep the peace. Others insisted that the tribes be allowed to protect their land at any and all cost. Although Spotted Tail knew firsthand the dangers of aggression against whites, he felt it was their only hope, and thus led the rallying cry for war . . .

Front Cover

Spotted Tail

by Charles A. Eastman

Nonfiction

The subject of the biography is:

What is the main time period of the biography?

Important facts about the biographical subject:

 **Plan**

After your preview, make a reading plan. Choose a strategy that can help you understand the key events of the subject's life and how they affected his or her personality.

• **Use the strategy of looking for cause and effect to help you understand how the subject's life experiences affected him or her.**

During Reading

D **Read with a Purpose**

Keep track of key events in the subject's life and what sort of effect they have. Record them on a Cause-Effect Organizer similar to the one below.

Directions: Do a careful reading of the excerpt from Spotted Tail's biography. Make notes on the Cause-Effect Organizer below.

Cause-Effect Organizer

Causes (Events)		Effects
	▶	
	▶	
	▶	

NAME ....

FOR USE WITH PAGES 193–209

from *Spotted Tail* by Charles A. Eastman

Among the Sioux chiefs of the "transition period" only one was shrewd enough to read coming events in their true light. It is said of Spotted Tail that he was rather a slow-moving boy, preferring in their various games and mimic battles to play the role of councilor, to plan and assign to the others their parts in the fray. This he did so cleverly that he soon became a leader among his youthful contemporaries; and withal he was apt at mimicry and impersonation, so that the other boys were accustomed to say of him, "He has his grandfather's wit and the wisdom of his grandmother!"

Spotted Tail was an orphan, reared by his grandparents, and at an early age compelled to fend for himself. Thus he was somewhat at a disadvantage among the other boys; yet even this fact may have helped to develop in him courage and ingenuity. One little incident of his youth, occurring at about his tenth year, is characteristic of the man. In the midst of a game, two boys became involved in a dispute which promised to be a serious one, as both drew knives. The young Spotted Tail instantly began to cry, "The Shoshones are upon us! To arms! To arms!" and the other boys joined in the war whoop. This distracted the attention of the combatants and ended the affair.

Stop and Organize
What can you say about Spotted Tail's personality?
Make notes on the Cause-Effect Organizer on page 86.

Upon the whole, his boyhood is not so well remembered as is that of most of his leading contemporaries, probably because he had no parents to bring him frequently before the people, as was the custom with the well-born, whose every step in their progress toward manhood was publicly announced at a feast given in their honor. It is known, however, that he began at an early age to carve out a position for himself. It is personal qualities alone that tell among our people, and the youthful Spotted Tail gained at every turn. At the age of seventeen, he had become a sure shot and a clever hunter, but, above all, he had already shown that he possessed a superior mind. He had come into contact with white people at the various trading posts, and according to his own story had made a careful study of the white man's habits and modes of thought, especially of his peculiar trait of economy and intense desire to accumulate property. He was accustomed to watch closely and listen attentively whenever any of this strange race had dealings with his people. When a council was held, and the other young men stood at a distance with their robes over their faces so as to avoid recognition, Spotted Tail always put himself in a position to hear all that was said on either side, and weighed all the arguments in his mind.

When he first went upon the warpath, it appears that he was, if anything, overzealous to establish himself in the eye of his people, and, as a matter of fact, it was especially hard for him to gain an assured position among the Brules, with whom he

Nonfiction

lived, both because he was an orphan and because his father had been of another band. Yet it was not long before he had achieved his ambition, though in doing so he received several ugly wounds. It was in a battle with the Utes that he first notably served his people and their cause.

The Utes were the attacking party and far outnumbered the Sioux on this occasion. Many of their bravest young men had fallen, and the Brules were face to face with utter annihilation, when Spotted Tail, with a handful of daring horsemen, dodged around the enemy's flank and fell upon them from the rear with so much spirit that it seemed that strong reinforcements had arrived, and the Utes retreated in confusion. The Sioux pursued on horseback; and it was in this pursuit that the noted chief Two Strike gained his historical name. But the honors of the fight belonged to Spotted Tail. The old chiefs, Conquering Bear and the rest, thanked him and at once made him a war chief.

Stop and Organize

What important events have you read about so far? Make notes on the Cause-Effect Organizer on page 86.

It had been the firm belief of Spotted Tail that it was unwise to allow the white man so much freedom in our country, long before the older chiefs saw any harm in it. After the opening of the Oregon Trail he, above all the others, was watchful of the conduct of the Americans as they journeyed toward the setting sun, and more than once he remarked in council that these white men were not like the French and the Spanish, with whom our old chiefs had been used to deal. He was not fully satisfied with the agreement with General Harney, but as a young warrior who had only just gained his position in the council, he could not force his views upon the older men.

No sooner had the Oregon Trail been secured from the Sioux than Fort Laramie and other frontier posts were strengthened, and the soldiers became more insolent and overbearing than ever. It was soon discovered that the whites were prepared to violate most of the articles of their treaty as the Indians understood it. At this time, the presence of many Mormon emigrants on their way to the settlements in Utah and Wyoming added to the perils of the situation, as they constantly maneuvered for purposes of their own to bring about a clash between the soldiers and the Indians. Every summer there were storm-clouds blowing between these two—clouds usually taking their rise in some affair of the travelers along the trail.

In 1854 an event occurred which has already been described and which snapped the last link of friendship between the races. By this time Spotted Tail had proved his courage both abroad and at home. He had fought a duel with one of the lesser chiefs, by whom he was attacked. He killed his opponent with an arrow, but himself received

◄ from *Spotted Tail* by Charles A. Eastman, continued ►

upon his head a blow from a battle-axe which brought him senseless to the ground. He was left for dead, but fortunately revived just as the men were preparing his body for burial.

The Brules sustained him in this quarrel, as he had acted in self-defense; and for a few years he led them in bloody raids against the whites along the historic trail. He ambushed many stagecoaches and emigrant trains, and was responsible for waylaying the Kincaid coach with twenty thousand dollars. This relentless harrying of travelers soon brought General Harney to the Brule Sioux to demand explanations and reparation.

The old chiefs of the Brules now appealed to Spotted Tail and his young warriors not to bring any general calamity upon the tribe. To the surprise of all, Spotted Tail declared that he would give himself up. He said that he had defended the rights of his people to the best of his ability, that he had avenged the blood of their chief, Conquering Bear, and that he was not afraid to accept the consequences. He therefore voluntarily surrendered to General Harney, and two of his lieutenants, Red Leaf and Old Woman, followed his example.

Thus Spotted Tail played an important part at the very outset of those events which were soon to overthrow the free life of his people. I do not know how far he foresaw what was to follow; but whether so conceived or not, his surrender was a master stroke, winning for him not only the admiration of his own people but the confidence and respect of the military.

Stop and Organize

What inferences can you make about Spotted Tail's personality?
Make notes on the Cause-Effect Organizer on page 86.

Using the Strategy

When reading a biography, it's important to think carefully about how the events of the subject's life affected his or her personality.

Directions: Return to the organizer on page 86. List events that affected Spotted Tail in the "causes" section. Make notes about the effects of these actions in the "effects" part of the organizer.

Nonfiction

Understanding How Biographies Are Organized

Good biographers include stories that help the reader form a strong impression of the subject.

- **Think of a biography as a series of stories that offer clues about the subject's personality.**

Directions: What is your impression of Spotted Tail? Make notes on this Character Web.

Character Web

Proof: ....

Proof: ....

Trait:

Trait:

Spotted Tail

Trait:

Trait:

Proof: ....

Proof: ....

NAME ....

E Connect

When you read a biography, think about your impression of the subject. Making a personal connection to an event or experience the author describes can help.

• **Record your own thoughts and feelings about the subject as you read.**

Directions: Reread this passage from the biography. Then complete the sticky note.

Connecting

The old chiefs of the Brules now appealed to Spotted Tail and his young warriors not to bring any general calamity upon the tribe. To the surprise of all, Spotted Tail declared that he would give himself up. He said that he had defended the rights of his people to the best of his ability, that he had avenged the blood of their chief, Conquering Bear, and that he was not afraid to accept the consequences. He therefore voluntarily surrendered to General Harney.

After Reading

When you finish a biography, think about what you've learned. Have you noted the events that shaped the subject's life?

F Pause and Reflect

Ask yourself questions about the biographical subject and your purpose for reading.

Directions: Complete the Looking Back chart on the following page with information about Spotted Tail.

Nonfiction

NAME ....

FOR USE WITH PAGES 193–209

Looking Back

Three important events in Spotted Tail's life	How these events may have affected his feelings about himself or others

G Reread

If you haven't formed a strong impression of the subject's life and personality, you need to do some rereading.

• **The rereading strategy of outlining can help you find and process additional details about the biographical subject.**

Directions: Reread key parts of the excerpt. Then write details about Spotted Tail on this Outline.

Outline

Spotted Tail
I. Early years
A. Important event:
B. Important event:
C. Important event:
II. Later years
A. Important event:
B. Important event:
C. Important event:

NAME

H Remember

Good readers remember what they've read. They also think about what they might read next. Making Study Cards can help.

• **Writing after you read can help you more easily retain what you've learned.**

Directions: Complete these Study Cards about the Spotted Tail reading.

Study Cards

Reading a Memoir

Most autobiographies tell the story of a writer's entire life. A memoir, in contrast, tells about just one part of the writer's life—very often a part that shaped the writer's life most significantly.

Before Reading

Here you'll use the reading process and the strategy of synthesizing to help you read a memoir about the tragic sinking of the ocean liner *Tuscania* during World War I.

A Set a Purpose

When you read a memoir, you look for information about the experience the writer describes. In addition, you'll also work to form your own impression of the writer and the people, places, times, and events.

• **To set your purpose, ask two questions about the writer of the memoir.**

Directions: Ask two questions about the sailor Irvin S. Cobb and his recollection of the sinking of the *Tuscania*.

Purpose question #1

....

....

....

Purpose question #2

....

....

....

NAME _____

B Preview

After you set your purpose, begin previewing. Watch for information that can help you meet your purpose.

Directions: Preview *When the Sea-Asp Stings*. Make notes on the stickies.

Back Cover

Because the *Tuscania* rode high out of the water and wallowed as she rode, because, during all those days of our crossing she hugged up close to our ship, splashing through the foam of our wake as though craving the comfort of our company, we called her things no self-respecting ship should have to bear. But when the other night we stood on the afterdeck of our ship, we running away as fast as our kicking screw would take us, and saw her going down, taking American soldier boys to death with her in alien waters, we drank toasts standing up to the poor old *Tuscania*.

—Irvin S. Cobb

Front Cover

WHEN THE SEA-ASP STINGS

BY IRVIN S. COBB

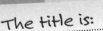

My questions: ....

The title is: ....

The quotation tells me: ....

C Plan

When you've finished previewing, make a reading plan that can help you meet your purpose.

- **Use the strategy of synthesizing to get a sense of the "big picture" the writer presents.**

During Reading

D Read with a Purpose

Your most important job when reading nonfiction is to find out as much as you can about the event or events the writer describes. Later, you'll think about the effect these events had on the writer.

Directions: Do a careful reading of *When the Sea-Asp Stings*. Make notes on this Key Topics Organizer as you read.

Key Topics Organizer

Key Topics	Notes from Reading
period the writer focuses on	
physical surroundings	
narrator	
narrative	
the other ship	
narrator's feeling	

NAME ....

FOR USE WITH PAGES 210–224

<table>
◆ from When the Sea-Asp Stings by Irvin S. Cobb ◆
</table>

Transatlantic journeys these days aren't what they used to be before America went into the war. Ours began to be different even before our ship pulled out from port. It is forbidden me to tell her name, and anyhow her name doesn't in the least matter, but she was a big ship with a famous skipper, and in peacetimes her sailing would have made some small stir. Instead we slipped away almost as if we had done something wrong. There was no waving of hands and handkerchiefs, no good-byes on the gangplanks, no rush to get back on land when the shore bell sounded. Alone and unescorted each one of us went soberly up the side of the ship, and then sundry hours later our journey began, as the ship, like a big gray ghost, slid away from land, as quietly as might be, into the congenial gray fog which instantly swallowed her up and left her in a little gray world of sea mist that was all her own. After this fashion, then, we started.

As for the first legs of the trip, they were much like the first legs of almost any sea trip except that we traveled in a convoy with sundry other ships, with war craft to guard us on our way. Our ship was quite full of soldiers—officers in the first cabin, and the steerage packed with khakied troopers—ninety percent of whom had never smelled bilge water before they embarked upon their great adventure overseas. There were fewer civilians than one formerly might have found on a ship bound for Europe. In these times only those civilians who have urgent business in foreign climes venture to go abroad.

Stop and Organize

Make some notes about the memoir on your Key Topics Organizer on page 96.

Except for a touch of seriousness about the daily lifeboat drill, and except that regimental discipline went forward, with the troops drilling on the open deck spaces when the weather and the sea permitted, there was at first nothing about this voyage to distinguish it from any other mid-winter voyage. Strangers got acquainted one with another and swapped views on politics, religion, symptoms, and Germans; flirtations started and ripened furiously; concerts were organized and took place, providing to be what concerts at sea usually are. Twice a day the regimental band played, and once a day, up on the bridge, the second officer took the sun, squinting into his sextant with the deep absorption with which in happier times a certain type of tourist was wont to stare through an enlarging crevice at a certain type of Parisian photograph. At night, though, we were in a darkened ship, a gilding black shape upon black waters, with heavy shades over all the portholes and thick draperies over all the doors, and only dim lights burning in the passageways and cross halls, so that every odd corner on deck or within was as dark as a coal pocket.

Nonfiction

from *When the Sea-Asp Stings* by Irvin S. Cobb, continued

When I emerged from [a bout of seasickness] it was to learn that we had reached the so-called danger zone. The escort of war craft for our transport had been augmented. By request the civilian passengers were expected to carry their life preservers with them wherever they went; but some of them forgot the injunction. I know I did frequently.

Our Captain no longer came to the saloon for his meals. He lived upon the bridge—ate there and, I think, slept there too—what sleeping he did. Standing there all muffled in his oilskins he looked even more of a squatty and unheroic figure than he had in his naval blue presiding at the head of the table; but by repute we knew him for a man who had gone through one torpedoing with great credit to himself and through numbers of narrow escapes, and we valued him accordingly and put our faith in him. It was faith well placed, as shall presently transpire.

I should not say that there was much fear aboard; at least if there was it did not manifest itself in the manner or the voice or the behavior of a single passenger seen by me; but there was a sort of nagging, persistent sense of uneasiness betraying itself in various small ways. For one thing, all of us made more jokes about submarines, mines, and other perils of the deep than was natural. There was something a little forced, artificial, about this gaiety—laughs came from the lips, but not from points further south.

We knew by hearsay that the *Tuscania* was a troopship bearing some of our soldiers over to do their share of the job of again making this world a fit place for human beings to live in. There was something pathetic in the fashion after which she so persistently and constantly strove to stick as closely under our stern as safety and the big waves would permit. It was as though her skipper placed all reliance in our skipper, looking to him to lead his ship out of peril should peril befall. Therefore, we of our little group watched her from our afterdecks, with her sharp nose forever half or wholly buried in the creaming white smother we kicked up behind us.

Stop and Organize

Make some notes on your Key Topics Organizer on page 96.

It was a crisp bright February day when we neared the coasts of the British Empire. At two o'clock in the afternoon we passed, some hundreds of yards to starboard, a round, dark, bobbing object which some observers thought was a floating mine. Others thought it might be the head and shoulders of a human body held upright in a life ring. Whatever it was, our ship gave it a wide berth, sheering off from the object in a sharp swing. Almost at the same moment upon our other bow, at a distance of not more than one hundred yards from the crooked course we were then pursuing, there appeared out through one of the swells a lifeboat, oarless, abandoned, empty, except for what looked like a woman's cloak lying across the thwarts. Rising

from *When the Sea-Asp Stings* by Irvin S. Cobb, continued

and falling to the swing of the sea it drifted down alongside of us so that we could look almost straight down into it. We did not stop to investigate but kept going, zigzagging as we went, and that old copy cat of a *Tuscania* came zigzagging behind us. A good many persons decided to tie on their life preservers.

Winter twilight was drawing on when we sighted land—Northern Ireland it was. The wind was going down with the sun and the sharp crests of the waves were dulling off, and blunt oily rollers began to splash with greasy sounds against our plates. Far away somewhere we saw the revolving light of a lighthouse winking across the face of the waters like a drunken eye. That little beam coming and going gave me a feeling of security. I was one of a member of the group for a farewell card game.

Perhaps an hour later, as we sat there intently engaged upon the favored indoor American sport of trying to better two pairs, we heard against our side of the ship a queer knocking sound rapidly repeated—a sound that somewhat suggested a boy dragging a stick along a picket fence.

"I suppose that's a torpedo knocking for admission," said one of us, looking up from his card and listening with a cheerful grin on his face.

I think it was not more than five minutes after that when an American officer opened the stateroom door and poked his head in.

"Better come along, you fellows," he said; "but come quietly so as not to give alarm or frighten any of the women. Something has happened. The *Tuscania*—she's in trouble."

Stop and Organize
Make some more notes on your Key Topics Organizer on page 96.

Up we got and hurried aft down the decks each one taking with him his cork jacket and adjusting it over his shoulders as he went. We came to the edge of the promenade deck aft. There were not many persons there, as well as we could tell in the thick darkness through which we felt our way, and not many more came afterward—in all I should say not more than seventy-five. All the rest were in ignorance of what had occurred—a good many were at dinner. Accounts of the disaster which I have read since my arrival in London said that the torpedo from the U-boat thudded into the vitals of the *Tuscania*, disarranged her engines, and left her in utter darkness for a while until her crew could switch on the auxiliary dynamo. I think this must have been a mistake, for at the moment of our reaching the deck of our ship the Tuscania was lighted up all over. Her illumination seemed especially brilliant, but that, I suppose, was largely because we had become accustomed to seeing our fellow transports as dark hulks at night.

I should say she was not more than a mile from us, almost due aft and a trifle to the left. But in the winter evening the distance increased each passing moment, for we were running away from her as fast as our engines could drive us. We could feel our

from *When the Sea-Asp Stings* by Irvin S. Cobb, continued

ship throb under our feet as she picked up speed. It made us feel like cowards. Near at hand a ship was in distress, a ship laden with a precious freightage of American soldier boys, and here we were legging it like a frightened bird, weaving in and out on sharp tacks.

We knew, of course, that we were under orders to get safely away if we could in case one of those sea adders, the submarines, should attack our convoy. We knew that guardian destroyers would even now be hurrying to the rescue, and we knew land was not many miles away, but all the same, I think I never felt such an object of shame as I felt that first moment when the realization dawned on me that we were fleeing from a stricken vessel instead of hastening back to give what succor we could.

As I stood there in the darkness, with silent, indistinct shapes all about me, it came upon me with almost the shock of a physical blow that the rows of lights I saw yonder through the murk were all slanting somewhat downward on what would be the bow of the disabled steamer. These oblique lines of light told the story. The *Tuscania* had been struck forward and was settling by the head.

Suddenly a little subdued "Ah! Ah!" burst like a chorus from us all. A red rocket—a rocket as red as blood—sprang up high into the air above those rows of lights. It hung aloft for a moment, then burst into a score of red balls, which fell, dimming out as they descended. After a bit two more rockets followed in rapid succession. Never again will a red rocket fired at night be to me anything except a reminder of the most pitiable, the most heart-racking thing I have ever seen—that poor appeal for help from the sinking *Tuscania* flaming against that foreign sky.

There was silence among us as we watched. None of us, I take it, had words within him to express what he felt; so we said nothing at all, but just stared out across the waters until our eyeballs ached in their sockets. So quiet were we that I jumped when right at my elbow a low, steady voice spoke. Turning my head I could make out the speaker was one of the younger American officers.

"If what I heard before we sailed is true," he said, "my brother is in the outfit on that boat yonder. Well, if they get him it will only add a little more interest to the debt I already owe those damned Germans."

Fifteen minutes passed, then twenty, then twenty-five. Now instead of many small lights we could make out only a few faint pin pricks of light against the blackness to mark the spot where the foundering vessel must be. Presently we could distinguish but one speck of light.

Still silent, we went below. Those of us who had not yet dined went and dined. Very solemnly, like men performing a rite, we ordered wine and we drank to the *Tuscania* and her British crew and her living cargo of American soldiers.

Stop and Organize
Make some final notes on your Key Topics Organizer on page 96.

NAME ....

Using the Strategy

Use the strategy of synthesizing to help you "see" the portrait the writer has created.

Directions: Think about your impression of Irvin S. Cobb. Then complete this Web.

◄ **Web**

Proof:

Proof:

Proof:

Trait:

Trait:

IRVIN S. COBB

Proof:

Trait:

Proof:

Proof:

Proof:

Nonfiction

Understanding How a Memoir Is Organized

Most memoir writers use chronological order as their organizing principle. Making Sequence Notes as you read can help you keep track of the major events or experiences the writer describes.

Directions: Record key events from Cobb's life on this organizer.

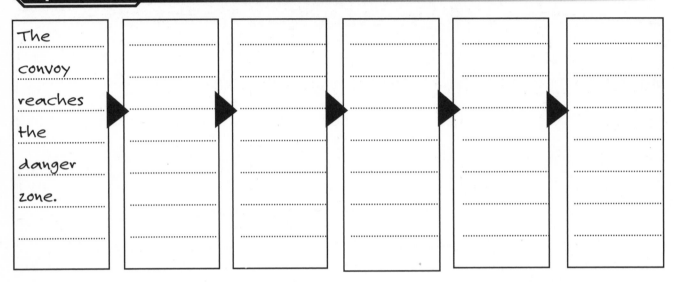

Sequence Notes

The convoy reaches the danger zone.

E Connect

Once you understand the events the writer describes, you can begin making inferences about the writer himself or herself.

• **Making a connection to a memoir means considering your impression of the writer.**

Directions: On the lines below, write your impression of Irvin S. Cobb. Support your ideas with proof from the excerpt.

Making Connections

After Reading

Take the time now to think about what you've learned.

F Pause and Reflect

At this point, you'll want to return to your reading purpose and think about whether you've accomplished what you set out to do.

- **After you finish a memoir, ask yourself, "How well did I meet my purpose?"**

Directions: Answer these questions about Irvin S. Cobb.

Looking Back

Have I been able to form an impression of the writer?

Do I have a clear understanding of the people, places, times, and events the writer describes?

Do I understand the purpose of the memoir?

G Reread

Some memoirs may raise as many questions as they answer. When this happens, you'll want to do some additional reading to find out more about the author or the subject he or she writes about.

- **Use the strategy of visualizing and thinking aloud to help you process information from a reading.**

Directions: Read the background information on the *Tuscania* below and on the next page. Then record your thoughts in the Think Aloud.

Nonfiction

The *Tuscania's* Final Trip

The *Tuscania*, which was built in 1914, was a passenger ship owned by the Cunard shipping company. On its maiden voyage and on every voyage thereafter, the *Tuscania* ferried Americans between New York City and Glasgow. When the United States entered World War I, the *Tuscania* was commissioned by the U.S. army to carry American soldiers back and forth to Glasgow.

In January 1918, the *Tuscania* joined a convoy of several other ships bound for Le Havre, France. After three weeks at sea, the convoy was sighted by the German submarine UB-77. At 5:40 p.m. on February 5, Lt. Commander Wilhelm Meyer ordered the crew of the UB-77 to fire upon the *Tuscania* and the other ships in the convoy. The second missile fired narrowly missed a large U.S. destroyer and hit the *Tuscania* broadside. Almost immediately, the captain of the *Tuscania* gave the order to abandon ship. With the help of other boats in the area, the majority of the *Tuscania's* passengers made it safely onto lifeboats, although some 230 soldiers and crew remained on deck as the ship sank.

The *Tuscania* was the first ship carrying American troops to be sunk during World War I. Avenging this loss of life became a top priority in the American fight against Germany.

Think Aloud

....

....

....

....

 Remember

Always find a way to remember what you've read.

• **Writing a review can help you retain what you've learned.**

Directions: Write a review of Cobb's account of the sinking of the *Tuscania*. Tell whether you'd recommend his memoir to others.

Book Review

....

....

....

....

Focus on Persuasive Writing

Good persuasive writing contains an assertion, support for the assertion, and a recommendation.

Step 1: Find the topic.

First, figure out the topic. Ask yourself, "What is the writer mostly talking about?"

Directions: Read this letter to the editor. Write your thoughts on the sticky note.

Eastern Ballet Bankruptcy: What You Can Do

To the Editor:

Last week, our city's beloved Eastern Ballet Company announced its bankruptcy. EBC's Board of Directors has put the company up for sale, and several cities around the country have expressed interest. My question for the people of our fair city is this: Why have we turned our back on EBC, one of the most prestigious ballet companies in America? Other cities recognize the value of our ballet company—so why don't we?

Over the last two years, the EBC Board has held numerous fundraisers in an attempt to keep the company solvent. Unfortunately, the board's pleas for funds were treated with a terrible indifference. Even an appeal to other arts organizations was ignored. No one, it seemed, was willing to pledge money to keep our dancers dancing. Finally, EBC's board gave up and took the long walk to bankruptcy court.

So now, our city may lose its ballet company. We'll have to travel elsewhere for *The Nutcracker* in December, *Swan Lake* in May, and *Romeo and Juliet* in September. Is this really what we want?

I believe we have one last shot at saving the EBC. What we need to do is show the EBC Board of Directors that our city really does care, and that we're willing to put our money where our mouths are. Take a moment now and sign a check made out to the Eastern Ballet Company. Send your contribution today to keep our beloved ballet company and its dancers here, where they belong.

Step 2: Find the assertion and support.

The assertion is a statement of belief that the writer explains and then supports.

Directions: Reread the letter. Write the author's assertion on the lines below. Then go back and highlight the author's support for the assertion.

The writer's assertion is

....

....

Step 3: Find the recommendation.

The recommendation is the action the writer wants you to take.

Directions: Circle the writer's recommendation in the letter to the editor you just read.

Step 4: Evaluate the argument.

As a final step, decide how you feel about the argument.

Directions: Complete the following Argument Chart. Write the assertion and support. Then evaluate the argument.

Argument Chart

Assertion	Support	My Opinion

Focus on  Speeches

Use the reading process to help you understand and respond to a speaker's message.

Step 1: Learn about the speaker.

Your first step will be to find out what you can about the speaker and why he or she is making the speech.

Directions: Read this speech. Make notes on the Web that follows.

from "Child Labor and Women's Suffrage" by Florence Kelley

Florence Kelley was a social reformer who fought long and hard for voting rights for women. In this speech, which she gave in Philadelphia in 1905, Kelley argues that if women were given the vote, the child labor problem would be solved.

We have, in this country, two million children under the age of sixteen years who are earning their bread. They vary in age from six and seven years (in the cotton mills of Georgia) and eight, nine, and ten years (in the coal-breakers of Pennsylvania), to fourteen, fifteen, and sixteen years in more enlightened states. . . .

Tonight while we sleep, several thousand little girls will be working in textile mills, all the night through, in the deafening noise of the spindles and the looms spinning and weaving cotton and wool, silks and ribbons for us to buy.

In Alabama the law provides that a child under sixteen years of age shall not work in a cotton mill at night longer than eight hours, and Alabama does better in this respect than any other southern state. North and South Carolina and Georgia place no restriction upon the work of children at night; and while we sleep little girls will be working tonight in the mills in those states, working eleven hours at night.

In Georgia there is no restriction whatever! A girl of six or seven years, just tall enough to reach the bobbins, may work eleven hours by day or by night. And they will do so tonight, while we sleep. . . .

If the mothers and the teachers in Georgia could vote, would the Georgia Legislature have refused at every session for the last three years to stop the work in the mills of children under twelve years of age? . . .

The children make our shoes in the shoe factories; they knit our stockings, our knitted underwear in the knitting factories. They spin and weave our cotton underwear in the cotton mills. Children braid straw for our hats, they spin and weave the silk and velvet wherewith we trim our hats. They stamp buckles and metal

from "Child Labor and Women's Suffrage" by Florence Kelley, continued

ornaments of all kinds, as well as pins and hat-pins. Under the sweating system, tiny children make artificial flowers and neckwear for us to buy. They carry bundles of garments from the factories to the tenements, little beasts of burden, robbed of school life that they may work for us. . . .

What can we do to free our consciences? There is one line of action by which we can do much. We can enlist the workingmen on behalf of our enfranchisement[1] just . . . as we strive with them to free the children. No labor organization in this country ever fails to respond to an appeal for help in the freeing of the children.

For the sake of the children, for the Republic in which these children will vote after we are dead, and for the sake of our cause, we should enlist the workingmen voters, with us, in this task of freeing the children from toil!

[1] **enfranchisement** the right to vote

Web

When

Where

Who

Florence kelley's speech

Why

What

Step 2: Reread.

Try to always read a speech at least twice. On your second reading, watch for key lines that clue you in as to the speaker's message.

Directions: Reread Florence Kelley's speech. Highlight the most important lines.

Step 3: Find the viewpoint.

The speaker's opinion, or main idea, is called the *viewpoint*. Use this formula to find the viewpoint:

Subject of the speech + Speaker's opinion of the subject = The speaker's main idea or viewpoint

Directions: Figure out the viewpoint of Kelley's speech.

Subject		Opinion		Main Idea
	+		=	

Step 4: Locate the support.

A good speaker will support his or her viewpoint with plenty of details.

Directions: Make notes about Florence Kelley's viewpoint and support on this Evidence Organizer.

Evidence Organizer

Viewpoint:			
Detail 1	Detail 2	Detail 3	Detail 4

Reading a Short Story

First and foremost, short stories are meant to be enjoyed. But the better you understand a story and its elements, the more you will enjoy it. The reading process can help.

Before Reading

Let the reading process and the strategy of synthesizing help you read and respond to "The Voyage," a short story by Katherine Mansfield.

A Set a Purpose

It's important to establish your purpose for reading a short story.

> • **Setting your purpose often involves asking questions about the plot and characters of a story.**

Directions: Think about the word *voyage*. What does it mean to you? Write your purpose questions for reading Mansfield's story.

Purpose Chart

Element	My Questions
characters	
setting	
plot	
dialogue	
point of view	

NAME ....

B Preview

You read better if you know what to expect. A preview can clue you in as to what's to come.

Directions: Preview "The Voyage." Then answer the questions and make a prediction about the story.

Who is the author of the story?
....

What did you find out about the point of view?
....

....

....

What did you learn from the first few paragraphs?
....

....

....

What repeated words did you notice?
....

....

My prediction:
....

....

....

....

```
"The Voyage" by Katherine Mansfield
```

What you need to know . . .

THE SELECTION In this story, a grandmother helps a lonely little girl take a voyage of the heart.

THE AUTHOR Katherine Mansfield (1888–1923) is one of the most celebrated short story writers of all time. She wrote "The Voyage" in the early 1920s, when she was at the height of her creative powers. It is considered one of her best stories.

LITERARY FOCUS characterization

FURTHER READING *The Garden Party*

"The Voyage" by Katherine Mansfield, continued

The Picton boat was due to leave at half-past eleven. It was a beautiful night, mild, starry, only when they got out of the cab and started to walk down the Old Wharf that jutted out into the harbor, a faint wind blowing off the water ruffled under Fenella's hat, and she put up her hand to keep it on. It was dark on the Old Wharf, very dark; the wool sheds, the cattle trucks, the cranes standing up so high, the little squat railway engine, all seemed carved out of solid darkness. Here and there on a rounded woodpile, that was like the stalk of a huge black mushroom, there hung a lantern, but it seemed afraid to unfurl its timid, quivering light in all that blackness; it burned softly, as if for itself.

Fenella's father pushed on with quick, nervous strides. Beside him her grandma bustled along in her crackling black ulster; they went so fast that she had now and again to give an undignified little skip to keep up with them. As well as her luggage strapped into a neat sausage, Fenella carried clasped to her her grandma's umbrella, and the handle, which was a swan's head, kept giving her shoulder a sharp little peck as if it too wanted her to hurry. Men, their caps pulled down, their collars turned up, swung by; a few women all muffled scurried along; and one tiny boy, only his little black arms and legs showing out of a white woolly shawl, was jerked along angrily between his father and mother; he looked like a baby fly that had fallen into the cream.

Then suddenly, so suddenly that Fenella and her grandma both leapt, there sounded from behind the largest wool shed, that had a trail of smoke hanging over it, "Mia-oo-oo-O-O!"

"First whistle," said her father briefly, and at that moment they came in sight of the Picton boat. Lying beside the dark wharf, all strung, all beaded with round golden lights, the Picton boat looked as if she was more ready to sail among stars than out into the cold sea. People pressed along the gangway. First went her grandma, then her father, then Fenella. There was a high step down on to the deck, and an old sailor in a jersey standing by gave her his dry, hard hand. They were there; they stepped out of the way of the hurrying people, and standing under a little iron stairway that led to the upper deck they began to say good-bye.

Stop and Organize
Make some notes in the Setting section of your Synthesizing Chart on page 119.

"There, mother, there's your luggage!" said Fenella's father, giving grandma another strapped-up sausage.

"Thank you, Frank."

"And you've got your cabin tickets safe?"

"Yes, dear."

"And your other tickets?"

◄ "The Voyage" by Katherine Mansfield, continued ►

Grandma felt for them inside her glove and showed him the tips.

"That's right." He sounded stern, but Fenella, eagerly watching him, saw that he looked tired and sad. "Mia-oo-oo-O-O!" The second whistle blared just above their heads, and a voice like a cry shouted, "Any more for the gangway?"

"You'll give my love to father," Fenella saw her father's lips say.

And her grandma, very agitated, answered, "Of course I will, dear. Go now. You'll be left. Go now, Frank. Go now."

"It's all right, mother. I've got another three minutes." To her surprise Fenella saw her father take off his hat. He clasped grandma in his arms and pressed her to him. "God bless you, mother!" she heard him say.

And grandma put her hand, with the black thread glove that was worn through on her ring finger, against his cheek, and she sobbed, "God bless you, my own brave son!"

This was so awful that Fenella quickly turned her back on them, swallowed once, twice, and frowned terribly at a little green star on a mast head. But she had to turn round again; her father was going.

"Good-bye, Fenella. Be a good girl." His cold, wet moustache brushed her cheek. But Fenella caught hold of the lapels of his coat.

"How long am I going to stay?" she whispered anxiously.

He wouldn't look at her. He shook her off gently, and gently said, "We'll see about that. Here! Where's your hand?" He pressed something into her palm. "Here's a shilling in case you should need it."

A shilling! She must be going away forever! "Father!" cried Fenella. But he was gone. He was the last off the ship. The sailors put their shoulders to the gangway. A huge coil of dark rope went flying through the air and fell "thump" on the wharf. A bell rang; a whistle shrilled. Silently the dark wharf began to slip, to slide, to edge away from them. Now there was a rush of water between. Fenella strained to see with all her might. "Was that father turning round?"—or waving?—or standing alone?—or walking off by himself? The strip of water grew broader, darker. Now the Picton boat began to swing round steady, pointing out to sea. It was no good looking any longer. There was nothing to be seen but a few lights, the face of the town clock hanging in the air, and more lights, little patches of them, on the dark hills.

Stop and Organize

Make some notes in the Style section of your Synthesizing Chart on page 119.

The freshening wind tugged at Fenella's skirts; she went back to her grandma. To her relief grandma seemed no longer sad. She had put the two sausages of luggage one on top of the other, and she was sitting on them, her hands folded, her head a little on one side. There was an intent, bright look on her face. Then Fenella saw that

"The Voyage" by Katherine Mansfield, continued

her lips were moving and guessed that she was praying. But the old woman gave her a bright nod as if to say the prayer was nearly over. She unclasped her hands, sighed, clasped them again, bent forward, and at last gave herself a soft shake.

"And now, child," she said, fingering the bow of her bonnet-strings, "I think we ought to see about our cabins. Keep close to me, and mind you don't slip."

"Yes, grandma!"

"And be careful the umbrellas aren't caught in the stair rail. I saw a beautiful umbrella broken in half like that on my way over."

"Yes, grandma."

Dark figures of men lounged against the rails. In the glow of their pipes a nose shone out, or the peak of a cap, or a pair of surprised-looking eyebrows. Fenella glanced up. High in the air, a little figure, his hands thrust in his short jacket pockets, stood staring out to sea. The ship rocked ever so little, and she thought the stars rocked too. And now a pale steward in a linen coat, holding a tray high in the palm of his hand, stepped out of a lighted doorway and skimmed past them. They went through that doorway. Carefully over the high brass-bound step on to the rubber mat and then down such a terribly steep flight of stairs that grandma had to put both feet on each step, and Fenella clutched the clammy brass rail and forgot all about the swan-necked umbrella.

At the bottom grandma stopped; Fenella was rather afraid she was going to pray again. But no, it was only to get out the cabin tickets. They were in the saloon. It was glaring bright and stifling; the air smelled of paint and burnt chop-bones and India rubber. Fenella wished her grandma would go on, but the old woman was not to be hurried. An immense basket of ham sandwiches caught her eye. She went up to them and touched the top one delicately with her finger.

"How much are the sandwiches?" she asked.

"Tuppence!" bawled a rude steward, slamming down a knife and fork.

Grandma could hardly believe it.

"Twopence each?" she asked.

"That's right," said the steward, and he winked at his companion.

Grandma made a small, astonished face. Then she whispered primly to Fenella. "What wickedness!" And they sailed out at the further door and along a passage that had cabins on either side. Such a very nice stewardess came to meet them. She was dressed all in blue, and her collar and cuffs were fastened with large brass buttons. She seemed to know grandma well.

"Well, Mrs. Crane," said she, unlocking their washstand. "We've got you back again. It's not often you give yourself a cabin."

"No," said grandma. "But this time my dear son's thoughtfulness—"

"I hope—" began the stewardess. Then she turned round and took a long, mournful look at grandma's blackness and at Fenella's black coat and skirt, black blouse, and hat with a crape rose.

Grandma nodded. "It was God's will," said she.

"The Voyage" by Katherine Mansfield, continued

Stop and Organize

Make some notes in the Plot section of your Synthesizing Chart on page 119.

The stewardess shut her lips and, taking a deep breath, she seemed to expand. "What I always say is," she said, as though it was her own discovery, "sooner or later each of us has to go, and that's a certainty." She paused. "Now, can I bring you anything, Mrs. Crane? A cup of tea? I know it's no good offering you a little something to keep the cold out."

Grandma shook her head. "Nothing, thank you. We've got a few wine biscuits, and Fenella has a very nice banana."

"Then I'll give you a look later on," said the stewardess, and she went out, shutting the door.

What a very small cabin it was! It was like being shut up in a box with grandma. The dark round eye above the washstand gleamed at them dully. Fenella felt shy. She stood against the door, still clasping her luggage and the umbrella. Were they going to get undressed in here? Already her grandma had taken off her bonnet, and, rolling up the strings, she fixed each with a pin to the lining before she hung the bonnet up. Her white hair shone like silk; the little bun at the back was covered with a black net. Fenella hardly ever saw her grandma with her head uncovered; she looked strange.

"I shall put on the woollen fascinator your dear mother crocheted for me," said grandma, and, unstrapping the sausage, she took it out and wound it round her head; the fringe of grey bobbles danced at her eyebrows as she smiled tenderly and mournfully at Fenella. Then she undid her bodice, and something under that, and something else underneath that. Then there seemed a short, sharp tussle, and grandma flushed faintly. Snip! Snap! She had undone her stays. She breathed a sigh of relief, and sitting on the plush couch, she slowly and carefully pulled off her elastic-sided boots and stood them side by side.

By the time Fenella had taken off her coat and skirt and put on her flannel dressing-gown grandma was quite ready.

"Must I take off my boots, grandma? They're lace." Grandma gave them a moment's deep consideration.

"You'd feel a great deal more comfortable if you did, child," said she. She kissed Fenella. "Don't forget to say your prayers. Our dear Lord is with us when we are at sea even more than when we are on dry land. And because I am an experienced traveller," said grandma briskly, "I shall take the upper berth."

"But, grandma, however will you get up there?"

Three little spider-like steps were all Fenella saw. The old woman gave a small silent laugh before she mounted them nimbly, and she peered over the high bunk at the astonished Fenella.

Fiction

"The Voyage" by Katherine Mansfield, continued

"You didn't think your grandma could do that, did you?" said she. And as she sank back Fenella heard her light laugh again.

The hard square of brown soap would not lather, and the water in the bottle was like a kind of blue jelly. How hard it was, too, to turn down those stiff sheets; you simply had to tear your way in. If everything had been different, Fenella might have got the giggles. . . . At last she was inside, and while she lay there panting, there sounded from above a long, soft whispering, as though some one was gently, gently rustling among tissue paper to find something. It was grandma saying her prayers.

A long time passed. Then the stewardess came in; she trod softly and leaned her hand on grandma's bunk.

"We're just entering the Straits," she said.

"Oh!"

"It's a fine night, but we're rather empty. We may pitch a little."

And indeed at that moment the Picton boat rose and rose and hung in the air just long enough to give a shiver before she swung down again, and there was the sound of heavy water slapping against her sides. Fenella remembered she had left the swan-necked umbrella standing up on the little couch. If it fell over, would it break? But grandma remembered too, at the same time.

"I wonder if you'd mind, stewardess, laying down my umbrella," she whispered.

"Not at all, Mrs. Crane." And the stewardess, coming back to grandma, breathed, "Your little granddaughter's in such a beautiful sleep."

"God be praised for that!" said grandma.

"Poor little motherless mite!" said the stewardess. And grandma was still telling the stewardess all about what happened when Fenella fell asleep.

Stop and Organize

Make some more notes in the Plot section of your Synthesizing Chart on page 119.

But she hadn't been asleep long enough to dream before she woke up again to see something waving in the air above her head. What was it? What could it be? It was a small grey foot. Now another joined it. They seemed to be feeling about for something; there came a sigh.

"I'm awake, grandma," said Fenella.

"Oh, dear, am I near the ladder?" asked grandma. "I thought it was at this end."

"No, grandma, it's the other. I'll put your foot on it. Are we there?" asked Fenella.

"In the harbour," said grandma. "We must get up, child. You'd better have a biscuit to steady yourself before you move."

But Fenella had hopped out of her bunk. The lamp was still burning, but night was over, and it was cold. Peering through that round eye she could see far off some

"The Voyage" by Katherine Mansfield, continued

rocks. Now they were scattered over with foam; now a gull flipped by; and now there came a long piece of real land.

"It's land, grandma," said Fenella, wonderingly, as though they had been at sea for weeks together. She hugged herself; she stood on one leg and rubbed it with the toes of the other foot; she was trembling. Oh, it had all been so sad lately. Was it going to change?

But all her grandma said was, "Make haste, child. I should leave your nice banana for the stewardess as you haven't eaten it." And Fenella put on her black clothes again and a button sprang off one of her gloves and rolled to where she couldn't reach it. They went up on deck.

Stop and Organize
Make some notes about grandma and Fenella in the Main Character section of your Synthesizing Chart on page 119.

But if it had been cold in the cabin, on deck it was like ice. The sun was not up yet, but the stars were dim, and the cold pale sky was the same color as the cold pale sea. On the land a white mist rose and fell. Now they could see quite plainly dark bush. Even the shapes of the umbrella ferns showed, and those strange silvery withered trees that are like skeletons. Now they could see the landing-stage and some little houses, pale too, clustered together, like shells on the lid of a box. The other passengers tramped up and down, but more slowly than they had the night before, and they looked gloomy.

And now the landing-stage came out to meet them. Slowly it swam towards the Picton boat, and a man holding a coil of rope, and a cart with a small drooping horse and another man sitting on the step, came too.

"It's Mr. Penreddy, Fenella, come for us," said grandma. She sounded pleased. Her white waxen cheeks were blue with cold, her chin trembled, and she had to keep wiping her eyes and her little pink nose.

"You've got my—"

"Yes, grandma."

Fenella showed it to her.

The rope came flying through the air, and "smack" it fell on to the deck. The gangway was lowered. Again Fenella followed her grandma on to the wharf over to the little cart, and a moment later they were bowling away. The hooves of the little horse drummed over the wooden piles, then sank softly into the sandy road. Not a soul was to be seen; there was not even a feather of smoke. The mist rose and fell and the sea still sounded asleep as slowly it turned on the beach.

"I seen Mr. Crane yestiddy," said Mr. Penreddy. "He looked himself then. Missus knocked him up a batch of scones last week."

"The Voyage" by Katherine Mansfield, continued

And now the little horse pulled up before one of the shell-like houses. They got down. Fenella put her hand on the gate, and the big, trembling dew-drops soaked through her glove-tips. Up a little path of round white pebbles they went, with drenched sleeping flowers on either side. Grandma's delicate white picotees were so heavy with dew that they were fallen, but their sweet smell was part of the cold morning. The blinds were down in the little house; they mounted the steps on to the veranda. A pair of old bluchers was on one side of the door, and a large red watering-can on the other.

"Tut! tut! Your grandpa," said grandma. She turned the handle. Not a sound. She called, "Walter!"

And immediately a deep voice that sounded half stifled called back, "Is that you, Mary?"

"Wait, dear," said grandma. "Go in there." She pushed Fenella gently into a small dusky sitting-room.

On the table a white cat, that had been folded up like a camel, rose, stretched itself, yawned, and then sprang on to the tips of its toes. Fenella buried one cold little hand in the white, warm fur, and smiled timidly while she stroked and listened to grandma's gentle voice and the rolling tones of grandpa.

A door creaked. "Come in, dear." The old woman beckoned, Fenella followed. There, lying to one side on an immense bed, lay grandpa. Just his head with a white tuft and his rosy face and long silver beard showed over the quilt. He was like a very old wide-awake bird.

"Well, my girl!" said grandpa. "Give us a kiss!" Fenella kissed him. "Ugh!" said grandpa. "Her little nose is as cold as a button. What's that she's holding? Her grandma's umbrella?"

Fenella smiled again, and crooked the swan neck over the bed-rail. Above the bed there was a big text in a deep black frame:—

"Lost! One Golden Hour
Set with Sixty Diamond Minutes.
No Reward Is Offered
For It Is Gone For Ever!"

"Yer grandma painted that," said grandpa. And he ruffled his white tuft and looked at Fenella so merrily she almost thought he winked at her.

Plan

Now choose a strategy that can help you keep track of the many literary elements that make up a story.

- **Synthesizing is like putting together the pieces of a jigsaw puzzle. In this case, the pieces are literary elements, and the puzzle is the story as a whole.**

During Reading

D Read with a Purpose

Directions: Now do your first reading of "The Voyage." Make notes on this organizer. If you need help, see pages 278–279 of the *Reader's Handbook*.

Synthesizing Chart

Literary Element	Most Important Aspect
Main Characters	
Setting	
Plot	
Style	
Theme	

Write facts from the story here.

Write your thoughts or the most important aspects here.

Fiction

Using the Strategy

There are many graphic organizers that can work with a short story.

- **A Story Organizer can help you reflect on the plot and theme of a story.**

Directions: Make notes about the plot and themes of "The Voyage" on this organizer.

Story Organizer

Beginning	Middle	End

Possible Theme

Understanding How Short Stories Are Organized

In most cases, the plot of a short story has five basic parts: exposition, rising action, climax, falling action, and resolution.

Directions: Use the Plot Diagram to show the organization of "The Voyage."

Plot Diagram

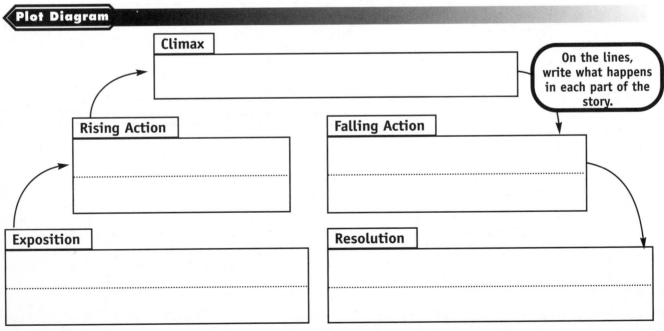

Connect

Making connections can enhance your enjoyment of a short story.

- **Use a Making Connections Chart to think through your connections to a story.**

<u>Directions:</u> Complete this chart for "The Voyage."

Making Connections Chart

I wonder why . . .	
I think . . .	
This is similar to . . .	
This reminds me of . . .	

After Reading

 Pause and Reflect

Always take a moment to reflect on the ending of the story.

- **After you finish a story, ask yourself, "Did things turn out the way I expected?"**

<u>Directions:</u> Answer the questions about "The Voyage."

Did the predictions you made about the story before reading turn out to be true?

....

....

How did you feel as you were reading the end of the story?

....

....

....

....

Fiction

Reread

When you do a second reading of a story, you'll probably pick up on things you missed the first time around. This can be important if you're having trouble understanding the story.

- **A powerful rereading strategy to use with short stories is close reading.**

Directions: Read the quotations on the Double-entry Journal organizer and then skim the story to find where the quotes appear. Write your response to each quotation.

Double-entry Journal

Text of "The Voyage"	What I think about it
This was so awful that Fenella quickly turned her back on them.	
The old woman gave a small silent laugh before she mounted them nimbly, and she peered over the high bunk at the astonished Fenella.	
Oh, it had all been so sad lately. Was it going to change?	

Remember

Sharing a story can help you remember it.

> • **To remember a story, discuss key aspects of the plot, characters, and theme.**

<u>**Directions:**</u> Get together in a small group to discuss "The Voyage." Use the discussion prompts below and write one of your own. Make notes about group members' answers.

Discussion Prompts

What is Fenella like at the beginning of the story?
How is she different at the end?
My discussion question:

Reading a Novel

You should use the reading process with all novels, especially with those that are long or complex. The reading process will guide you through even the most challenging works.

Before Reading

Here you'll practice using the reading process and the strategy of using graphic organizers with an excerpt from the classic novel *Tarzan of the Apes*.

 A Set a Purpose

If you're reading the novel for a school assignment, at least a part of your purpose will be to learn what you can about important literary elements in the novel, including point of view, characters, setting, plot, and theme.

• **To set your purpose, ask questions about the major literary elements of the novel.**

Directions: You will be reading Chapter 3 of Edgar Rice Burroughs's *Tarzan of the Apes*. Write your purpose questions on the chart below. (We've done the first one for you.)

Purpose Chart

Element	My Questions
point of view	From whose perspective is the story told?
characters	
setting	
plot	
theme	

B Preview

Always begin with a preview of the novel. Pay particular attention to the front and back covers.

Directions: Preview the front and back covers of *Tarzan of the Apes*. Write important facts and details on the sticky notes.

Back Cover

Presenting the first novel of Edgar Rice Burroughs's enormously popular Tarzan series . . .

Published in 1914 and set in the late 1800s, *Tarzan of the Apes* is the story of a boy who is born in the jungle and raised by a family of apes as one of their own.

Tarzan of the Apes opens with the story of the baby's parents—Lord and Lady Greystoke—who are left to die on a jungle island by a ship's mutinous crew. After several months on the island, Lady Greystoke gives birth to a baby boy. Unbeknownst to his mother and father, this tiny and beloved "man-child" will grow up to become the all-powerful "Tarzan, King of the Jungle."

Front Cover

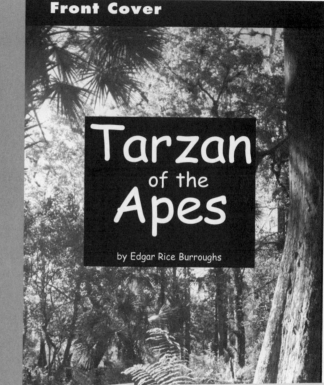

Tarzan of the Apes

by Edgar Rice Burroughs

Fiction

Important information about the book:

....

....

....

....

Details that relate to my purpose:

....

....

....

....

The title is:

....

The author is:

....

....

Plan

The best reading strategy to employ with novels is using graphic organizers. Become an expert on the organizers that work best for you.

• **Good readers know that using graphic organizers can help them get more from a novel.**

Directions: Make notes on this Fiction Organizer as you read Chapter 3 of *Tarzan of the Apes*.

Fiction Organizer

Characters

Setting

Theme

Tarzan of the Apes, Chapter 3

Point of View

Plot

NAME ....

During Reading

D Read with a Purpose

Use a Fiction Organizer to sort information about literary elements in a novel.

Directions: Now do a careful reading of Chapter 3 of *Tarzan of the Apes*. Make notes about point of view, characters, setting, plot, and theme.

> from *Tarzan of the Apes* by Edgar Rice Burroughs

Chapter 3: Life and Death

Morning found them but little, if at all, refreshed, though it was with a feeling of intense relief that they saw the day dawn.

As soon as they had made their meager breakfast of salt pork, coffee, and biscuit, Clayton commenced work upon their house, for he realized that they could hope for no safety and no peace of mind at night until four strong walls effectually barred the jungle life from them.

The task was an arduous one and required the better part of a month, though he built but one small room. He constructed his cabin of small logs about six inches in diameter, stopping the chinks with clay which he found at the depth of a few feet beneath the surface soil.

At one end he built a fireplace of small stones from the beach. These also he set in clay and when the house had been entirely completed he applied a coating of the clay to the entire outside surface to the thickness of four inches.

In the window opening he set small branches about an inch in diameter both vertically and horizontally, and so woven that they formed a substantial grating that could withstand the strength of a powerful animal. Thus they obtained air and proper ventilation without fear of lessening the safety of their cabin.

The A-shaped roof was thatched with small branches laid close together and over these long jungle grass and palm fronds, with a final coating of clay.

The door he built of pieces of the packing-boxes which had held their belongings, nailing one piece upon another, the grain of contiguous layers running transversely, until he had a solid body some three inches thick and of such great strength that they were both moved to laughter as they gazed upon it.

Here the greatest difficulty confronted Clayton, for he had no means whereby to hang his massive door now that he had built it. After two days' work, however, he succeeded in fashioning two massive hardwood hinges, and with these he hung the door so that it opened and closed easily.

The stuccoing and other final touches were added after they moved into the house, which they had done as soon as the roof was on, piling their boxes before the door at night and thus having a comparatively safe and comfortable habitation.

Fiction

from *Tarzan of the Apes* by Edgar Rice Burroughs, continued

Stop and Organize

What is the story's setting? From whose point of view is the story told?
Make notes on your Fiction Organizer on page 126.

The building of a bed, chairs, table, and shelves was a relatively easy matter, so that by the end of the second month they were well settled, and, but for the constant dread of attack by wild beasts and the ever growing loneliness, they were not uncomfortable or unhappy.

At night great beasts snarled and roared about their tiny cabin, but, so accustomed may one become to oft repeated noises, that soon they paid little attention to them, sleeping soundly the whole night through.

Thrice had they caught fleeting glimpses of great man-like figures like that of the first night, but never at sufficiently close range to know positively whether the half-seen forms were those of man or brute.

The brilliant birds and the little monkeys had become accustomed to their new acquaintances, and as they had evidently never seen human beings before they presently, after their first fright had worn off, approached closer and closer, impelled by that strange curiosity which dominates the wild creatures of the forest and the jungle and the plain, so that within the first month several of the birds had gone so far as even to accept morsels of food from the friendly hands of the Claytons.

One afternoon, while Clayton was working upon an addition to their cabin, for he contemplated building several more rooms, a number of their grotesque little friends came shrieking and scolding through the trees from the direction of the ridge. Ever as they fled they cast fearful glances back of them, and finally they stopped near Clayton jabbering excitedly to him as though to warn him of approaching danger.

At last he saw it, the thing the little monkeys so feared—the man-brute of which the Claytons had caught occasional fleeting glimpses.

It was approaching through the jungle in a semi-upright position, now and then placing the backs of its closed fists upon the ground—a great anthropoid ape, and, as it advanced, it emitted deep guttural growls and an occasional low barking sound.

Clayton was at some distance from the cabin, having come to fell a particularly perfect tree for his building operations. Grown careless from months of continued safety, during which time he had seen no dangerous animals during the daylight hours, he had left his rifles and revolvers all within the little cabin, and now that he saw the great ape crashing through the underbrush directly toward him, and from a direction which practically cut him off from escape, he felt a vague little shiver play up and down his spine.

from *Tarzan of the Apes* by Edgar Rice Burroughs, continued

He knew that, armed only with an ax, his chances with this ferocious monster were small indeed—and Alice; O God, he thought, what will become of Alice?

There was yet a slight chance of reaching the cabin. He turned and ran toward it, shouting an alarm to his wife to run in and close the great door in case the ape cut off his retreat.

Lady Greystoke had been sitting a little way from the cabin, and when she heard his cry she looked up to see the ape springing with almost incredible swiftness, for so large and awkward an animal, in an effort to head off Clayton.

With a low cry she sprang toward the cabin, and, as she entered, gave a backward glance which filled her soul with terror, for the brute had intercepted her husband, who now stood at bay grasping his ax with both hands ready to swing it upon the infuriated animal when he should make his final charge.

"Close and bolt the door, Alice," cried Clayton. "I can finish this fellow with my ax."

But he knew he was facing a horrible death, and so did she.

The ape was a great bull, weighing probably three hundred pounds. His nasty, close-set eyes gleamed hatred from beneath his shaggy brows, while his great canine fangs were bared in a horrid snarl as he paused a moment before his prey.

Over the brute's shoulder Clayton could see the doorway of his cabin, not twenty paces distant, and a great wave of horror and fear swept over him as he saw his young wife emerge, armed with one of his rifles.

She had always been afraid of firearms, and would never touch them, but now she rushed toward the ape with the fearlessness of a lioness protecting its young.

"Back, Alice," shouted Clayton, "for God's sake, go back."

Stop and Organize
What inferences can you make about Clayton?
Make notes on your Fiction Organizer on page 126.

But she would not heed, and just then the ape charged, so that Clayton could say no more.

The man swung his ax with all his mighty strength, but the powerful brute seized it in those terrible hands, and tearing it from Clayton's grasp hurled it far to one side.

With an ugly snarl he closed upon his defenseless victim, but ere his fangs had reached the throat they thirsted for, there was a sharp report and a bullet entered the ape's back between his shoulders.

Throwing Clayton to the ground the beast turned upon his new enemy. There before him stood the terrified girl vainly trying to fire another bullet into the animal's body; but she did not understand the mechanism of the firearm, and the hammer fell futilely upon an empty cartridge.

Fiction

from *Tarzan of the Apes* by Edgar Rice Burroughs, continued

Almost simultaneously Clayton regained his feet, and without thought of the utter hopelessness of it, he rushed forward to drag the ape from his wife's prostrate form.

With little or no effort he succeeded, and the great bulk rolled inertly upon the turf before him—the ape was dead. The bullet had done its work.

A hasty examination of his wife revealed no marks upon her, and Clayton decided that the huge brute had died the instant he had sprung toward Alice.

Gently he lifted his wife's still unconscious form, and bore her to the little cabin, but it was fully two hours before she regained consciousness.

Her first words filled Clayton with vague apprehension. For some time after regaining her senses, Alice gazed wonderingly about the interior of the little cabin, and then, with a satisfied sigh, said:

"O, John, it is so good to be really home! I have had an awful dream, dear. I thought we were no longer in London, but in some horrible place where great beasts attacked us."

"There, there, Alice," he said, stroking her forehead, "try to sleep again, and do not worry your head about bad dreams."

That night a little son was born in the tiny cabin beside the primeval forest, while a leopard screamed before the door, and the deep notes of a lion's roar sounded from beyond the ridge.

Lady Greystoke never recovered from the shock of the great ape's attack, and, though she lived for a year after her baby was born, she was never again outside the cabin, nor did she ever fully realize that she was not in England.

Stop and Organize

What inferences can you make about Alice?
Make notes on your Fiction Organizer on page 126.

Sometimes she would question Clayton as to the strange noises of the nights; the absence of servants and friends, and the strange rudeness of the furnishings within her room, but, though he made no effort to deceive her, never could she grasp the meaning of it all.

In other ways she was quite rational, and the joy and happiness she took in the possession of her little son and the constant attentions of her husband made that year a very happy one for her, the happiest of her young life.

That it would have been beset by worries and apprehension had she been in full command of her mental faculties Clayton well knew; so that while he suffered terribly to see her so, there were times when he was almost glad, for her sake, that she could not understand.

Long since had he given up any hope of rescue, except through accident. With unremitting zeal he had worked to beautify the interior of the cabin.

from *Tarzan of the Apes* by Edgar Rice Burroughs, continued

Skins of lion and panther covered the floor. Cupboards and bookcases lined the walls. Odd vases made by his own hand from the clay of the region held beautiful tropical flowers. Curtains of grass and bamboo covered the windows, and, most arduous task of all, with his meager assortment of tools he had fashioned lumber to neatly seal the walls and ceiling and lay a smooth floor within the cabin.

That he had been able to turn his hands at all to such unaccustomed labor was a source of mild wonder to him. But he loved the work because it was for her and the tiny life that had come to cheer them, though adding a hundredfold to his responsibilities and to the terribleness of their situation.

During the year that followed, Clayton was several times attacked by the great apes which now seemed to continually infest the vicinity of the cabin; but as he never again ventured outside without both rifle and revolvers he had little fear of the huge beasts.

He had strengthened the window protections and fitted a unique wooden lock to the cabin door, so that when he hunted for game and fruits, as it was constantly necessary for him to do to insure sustenance, he had no fear that any animal could break into the little home.

At first he shot much of the game from the cabin windows, but toward the end the animals learned to fear the strange lair from whence issued the terrifying thunder of his rifle.

Stop and Organize

What would you say are some of the big ideas or possible themes in this novel? Make notes on your Fiction Organizer on page 126.

In his leisure Clayton read, often aloud to his wife, from the store of books he had brought for their new home. Among these were many for little children—picture books, primers, readers—for they had known that their little child would be old enough for such before they might hope to return to England.

At other times Clayton wrote in his diary, which he had always been accustomed to keep in French, and in which he recorded the details of their strange life. This book he kept locked in a little metal box.

A year from the day her little son was born Lady Alice passed quietly away in the night. So peaceful was her end that it was hours before Clayton could awake to a realization that his wife was dead.

The horror of the situation came to him very slowly, and it is doubtful that he ever fully realized the enormity of his sorrow and the fearful responsibility that had devolved upon him with the care of that wee thing, his son, still a nursing babe.

The last entry in his diary was made the morning following her death, and there he recites the sad details in a matter-of-fact way that adds to the pathos of it; for it

from *Tarzan of the Apes* **by Edgar Rice Burroughs, continued**

breathes a tired apathy born of long sorrow and hopelessness, which even this cruel blow could scarcely awake to further suffering:

My little son is crying for nourishment—O Alice, Alice, what shall I do?

And as John Clayton wrote the last words his hand was destined ever to pen, he dropped his head wearily upon his outstretched arms where they rested upon the table he had built for her who lay still and cold in the bed beside him.

For a long time no sound broke the deathlike stillness of the jungle midday save the piteous wailing of the tiny man-child.

Stop and Organize

What happens in this chapter of the book? What are the key events? Make notes on your Fiction Organizer on page 126.

Using the Strategy

Skim the Reading Tools section of the *Reader's Handbook* for organizers that work well with fiction. An excellent one, for example, is a Character Map.

Directions: Make notes about Clayton on the following Character Map.

Character Map

How he acts	What he says

Clayton

What he thinks	What I've learned about him so far

Understanding How Novels Are Organized

Plots often proceed in chronological order. One event leads to another, and all events build toward the climax.

• **A Story String can help you track key events in a plot.**

Directions: Think about what happens in Chapter 3 of *Tarzan of the Apes*. Then make notes on the following Story String.

Story String

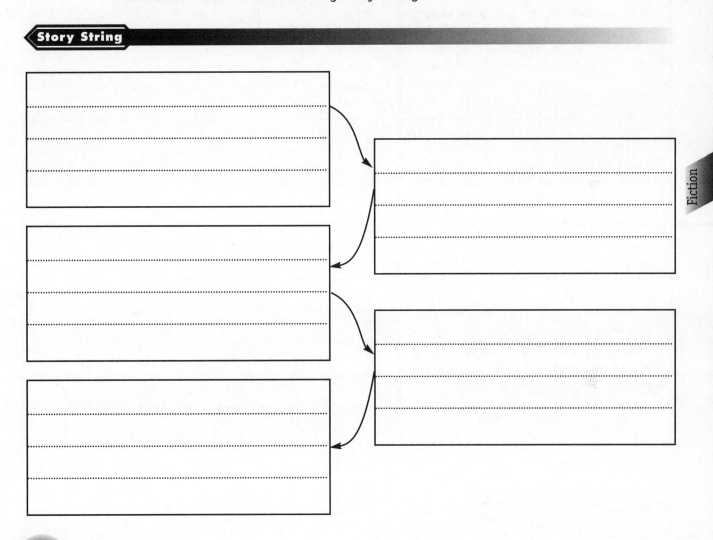

E Connect

Keep track of your reactions to events and characters in a novel. It can make the work easier to remember and more enjoyable to read.

• **Making connections with a novel means recording your thoughts and feelings about the text.**

Directions: Read the quotes from *Tarzan of the Apes* on the left of the following Double-entry Journal. Write how they make you feel or what they remind you of on the right side.

Fiction

Double-entry Journal

Quote	My Reaction
"He knew that, armed only with an ax, his chances with this ferocious monster were small indeed—and Alice; O God, he thought, what will become of Alice?"	
"And as John Clayton wrote the last words his hand was destined ever to pen, he dropped his head wearily upon his outstretched arms where they rested upon the table he had built for her who lay still and cold in the bed beside him."	
"For a long time no sound broke the deathlike stillness of the jungle midday save the piteous wailing of the tiny man-child."	

After Reading

F Pause and Reflect

Keep in mind that your original purpose was to find details about point of view, characters, setting, plot, and theme. If the novel is long, stop after each chapter or two and check your understanding of the various literary elements.

• **After you finish a novel, ask yourself, "How well did I meet my purpose?"**

Directions: Answer *yes* or *no* to each question about the chapter you read from *Tarzan of the Apes*.

NAME ....

Looking Back

Questions	My answer	What I need to understand better
Do I know the point of view?	yes no	
Do I have a strong understanding of the characters I've met thus far?	yes no	
Can I visualize the setting?	yes no	
Do I understand the plot up to this point?	yes no	
Have I begun to think about the big ideas or themes in the work?	yes no	

> If the novel is long, stop after each chapter or two and check your understanding of the various literary elements.

 Reread

If you haven't met your purpose, you may need to do some rereading. Rather than reread word for word, however, you'll want to skim chunks of the novel for clues about one of the major literary elements. The rereading strategy of synthesizing can help.

• **Use synthesizing to help you see how the parts of a novel fit together.**

Directions: Complete this Synthesizing Chart for Chapter 3 of *Tarzan of the Apes*. If you need help, see page 310 in the *Reader's Handbook*.

Synthesizing Chart

Literary Element	Most Important Aspect
Main Characters	
Setting	
Plot	
Theme	

Write facts from the story here.

Write your thoughts or the most important aspects here.

 Remember

Keep notes to help you remember what happens from one chapter to the next in a novel.

- **Writing a brief summary of each chapter can help you keep track of what happens throughout the novel.**

Directions: Write a brief summary of Chapter 3 of *Tarzan of the Apes*.

Summary

Tarzan of the Apes: Chapter 3

....

....

....

....

....

....

Focus on 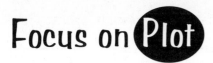 Plot

To understand a story, you must understand its plot. Practice reading the plot of this ancient Greek myth.

Step 1: Track the key events.

On your first reading, focus on the plot. Ask yourself, "Who's involved, and what are they doing?"

Directions: Read this myth. Underline key events.

"Pegasus and the Chimaera" by Thomas Bulfinch

When Perseus cut off Medusa's head, the blood sinking into the earth produced the winged horse Pegasus. Minerva caught and tamed him, and presented him to the Muses. The fountain Hippocrene, on the Muses' mountain Helicon, was opened by a kick from his hoof.

The Chimaera was a fearful monster, breathing fire. The fore part of its body was a compound of the lion and the goat, and the hind part a dragon's. It made great havoc in Lycia, so that the king Iobates sought for some hero to destroy it. At that time there arrived at his court a gallant young warrior, whose name was Bellerophon. He brought letters from Proetus, the son-in-law of Iobates, recommending Bellerophon in the warmest terms as an unconquerable hero, but added at the close a request to his father-in-law to put him to death. The reason was that Proetus was jealous of him, suspecting that his wife Antea looked with too much admiration on the young warrior.

Iobates, on perusing the letters, was puzzled what to do, not willing to violate the claims of hospitality, yet wishing to oblige his son-in-law. A lucky thought occurred to him, to send Bellerophon to combat with the Chimaera. Bellerophon accepted the proposal, but before proceeding to the combat consulted the soothsayer Polyidus, who advised him to procure if possible the horse Pegasus for the conflict. For this purpose he directed him to pass the night in the temple of Minerva. He did so, and as he slept Minerva came to him and gave him a golden bridle. When he awoke the bridle remained in his hand. Minerva also showed him Pegasus drinking at the well of Pirene, and at sight of the bridle, the winged steed came willingly and suffered himself to be taken. Bellerophon mounting, rose with him into the air, and soon found the Chimaera, and gained an easy victory over the monster.

Fiction

Step 2: Diagram the plot.

Use a Plot Diagram to help you understand the major parts of a plot.

Directions: Complete this Plot Diagram using key events from "Pegasus and the Chimaera."

◄ **Plot Diagram**

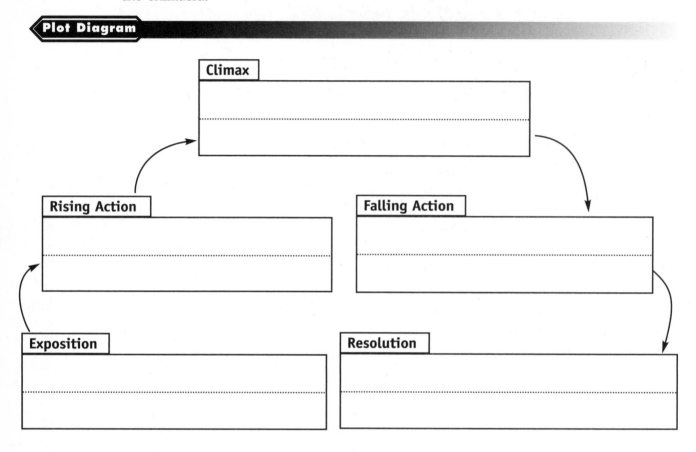

Step 3: Consider the climax.

The climax is the turning point in the action of a story.

Directions: Reread what you wrote on your Plot Diagram. Then discuss the climax of "Pegasus and the Chimaera."

....

....

....

....

....

Focus on Setting

When you focus on the setting, you carefully consider the time and place of a story and how it affects such elements as characters, plot, and mood.

Step 1: Do a close reading.

To find setting clues, read carefully and pay attention to each and every detail.

Directions: Read this paragraph from a short story. Underline clues about time. Highlight clues about place.

> ### from "Death of a Traveling Salesman" by Eudora Welty
>
> R. J. Bowman, who for fourteen years had traveled for a shoe company through Mississippi, drove his Ford along a rutted dirt path. It was a long day! The time did not seem to clear the noon hurdle and settle into soft afternoon. The sun, keeping its strength here and even in winter, stayed at the top of the sky, and every time Bowman stuck his head out of the dusty car to stare upon the road, it seemed to reach a long arm down and push against the top of his head, right through his hat—like the practical joke of an old drummer, long on the road. It made him feel all the more antsy and helpless. He was feverish, and he was not quite sure of the way.

My inferences about time:

....

....

....

....

....

....

....

How I know this:

....

....

....

....

....

....

....

....

....

....

....

....

My inferences about place:

....

....

....

....

How I know this:

....

....

....

....

....

....

Step 2: Draw conclusions about mood and character.

The setting of a story can make you feel a certain way or give you ideas about the characters. In other words, it can affect both mood and characterization.

Directions: Read these details about the setting. Then write your inferences about mood and character.

Inference Chart

Quotes from the Text	My Thoughts about Mood	My Thoughts about Character
"R. J. Bowman, who for fourteen years had traveled for a shoe company through Mississippi . . . "		
"The time did not seem to clear the noon hurdle and settle into soft afternoon."		
"It made him feel all the more antsy and helpless."		

Step 3: Make inferences about plot.

The setting can foreshadow or give hints about what's to come in the plot.

Directions: Make a prediction about what you think happens next in "Death of a Traveling Salesman."

My prediction:

Focus on Characters

An author reveals character through both dialogue and description. What the character says and thinks can give you important clues about the themes of the work.

Step 1: Read for character clues.

Directions: Read this excerpt from *Song of Solomon* about a character named Milkman. Underline what Milkman says and thinks. Highlight any other important details. Then make notes on the sticky.

> ### from *Song of Solomon* by Toni Morrison
>
> By the time Milkman was fourteen he had noticed that one of his legs was shorter than the other. When he stood barefoot and straight as a pole, his left foot was about half an inch off the floor. So he never stood straight; he slouched or leaned or stood with a hip thrown out, and he never told anybody about it ever. When Lena said, "Mama, what is he walking like that for?" he said, "I'll walk any way I want to, including over your ugly face." Ruth said, "Be quiet, you two. It's just growing pains, Lena." Milkman knew better. It wasn't a limp—not at all—just the suggestion of one, but it looked like an affected walk, the strut of a very young man trying to appear more sophisticated than he was. It bothered him and he acquired movements and habits to disguise what to him was a burning defect. He sat with his left ankle on his right knee, never the other way around. And he danced each new dance with a curious stiff-legged step that the girls loved and other boys eventually copied. The deformity was mostly in his mind. Mostly, but not completely, for he did have shooting pains in that leg after several hours on a basketball court. He favored it, believed it was polio, and felt secretly connected to the late President Roosevelt for that reason.

What I know about Milkman:

....

....

....

....

....

....

....

Fiction

Step 2: Make inferences.

Next, use the clues you've found to help you make inferences about the character.

Directions: Complete this Inference Chart about Milkman.

◀ **Inference Chart**

What the character says and thinks	What I can conclude about him
". . . he never told anybody about it ever."	
"I'll walk any way I want to, including over your ugly face."	
"He favored it, believed it was polio, and felt secretly connected to the late President Roosevelt for that reason."	

Step 3: Connect character to theme.

A character's thoughts and actions often can point the way to important themes in the work.

Directions: A "big idea" in *Song of Solomon* is self-worth. Make a connection between this idea and the character of Milkman. Write your ideas on the lines below.

"Big idea": self-worth ....

My ideas: ....

....

....

....

....

....

Focus on Theme

Theme is the statement about life that the author wants to convey in a work. The plot and characters of a story can provide clues about theme.

Step 1: Identify the central topics in the work.

To find the central topics, ask yourself: "What is the author mostly talking about?"

Directions: Reread this excerpt from *Lord of the Flies*, the story of a group of boys and what happens to them after their plane crashes on an uninhabited island. What do you think are the central topics in this work?

from *Lord of the Flies* by William Golding

They were in the beginnings of the thick forest, plonking with weary feet on a track, when they heard the noises—squeakings—and the hard strike of hoofs on a path. As they pushed forward the squeaking increased till it became a frenzy. They found a piglet caught in a curtain of creepers, throwing itself at the elastic traces in all the madness of extreme terror. Its voice was thin, needle-sharp and insistent. The three boys rushed forward and Jack drew his knife again with a flourish. He raised his arm in the air. There came a pause, a hiatus, the pig continued to scream and the creepers to jerk, and the blade continued to flash at the end of a bony arm. The pause was only long enough for them to understand what an enormity the downward stroke would be. Then the piglet tore loose from the creepers and scurried into the undergrowth. They were left looking at each other and the place of terror. Jack's face was white under the freckles. He noticed that he still held the knife aloft and brought his arm down replacing the blade in the sheath. Then they all three laughed ashamedly and began to climb back to the track.

The central topics

are:

....

....

....

Fiction

Step 2: Consider what the characters do or say.

Next, make a connection between the central topics and the characters of
the work.

Directions: Read these lines from *Lord of the Flies*. Tell how they relate to
the central topics you listed on the previous page.

Double-entry Journal

Quote	What I Think about It
"They found a piglet caught in a curtain of creepers, throwing itself at the elastic traces in all the madness of extreme terror."	
"The three boys rushed forward and Jack drew his knife again with a flourish."	
"The pause was only long enough for them to understand what an enormity the downward stroke would be."	
"Then they all three laughed ashamedly and began to climb back to the track."	

Step 3: Think about the point the author is making.

Remember that theme is the point the author is making about the central idea.

Directions: Use the information from Steps 1 and 2 to complete this organizer.

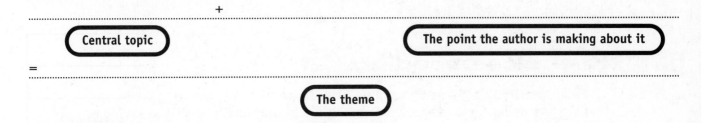

+

(Central topic)   (The point the author is making about it)

=

(The theme)

Step 4: Pull it all together.

After you identify a theme, find details in the work that support it.

Directions: Explore the theme of violence in *Lord of the Flies*. Make notes on the Topic and Theme Organizer below.

Topic and Theme Organizer

Topic:
....

Detail #1:
....

....

....

Detail #2:
....

....

....

Detail #3:
....

....

....

Theme:
....

....

....

Fiction

Focus on Dialogue

When you read dialogue, pay attention to who's speaking to whom and what they're talking about. Remember that dialogue gives important clues about character, plot, and mood.

Step 1: Do a close reading.

First, identify key pieces of dialogue. Use the strategy of close reading to help you understand what the characters are saying and how they're saying it.

Directions: Do a close reading of this piece of dialogue from a short story. Write your reactions on the sticky notes.

from "The Golden Honeymoon" by Ring Lardner

Mother says that when I start talking I never know when to stop. But I tell her the only time I get a chance is when she ain't around, so I have to make the most of it. I guess the fact is neither one of us would be welcome at a Quaker meeting, but as I tell Mother, what did God give us tongues for if He didn't want we should use them? Only she says, "He didn't give them to us to say the same thing over and over again," like I do, and repeat myself.

"Well, Mother," I say, "when people is like you and I and been married fifty years, do you expect everything I say will be something you ain't heard me say before? But it may be new to others, as they ain't nobody else lived with me as long as you have."

So she says:

"You can bet they ain't, as they couldn't nobody else stand you that long."

"Well," I tell her, "you look pretty healthy."

"Maybe I do," she will say, "but I looked even healthier before I married you."

You can't get ahead of Mother.

This conversation is between _____ and _____

_____

_____

They are talking about _____

_____

_____

This is how the characters sound:

_____

_____

_____

_____

Step 2: Look for clues about character.

Next, read for character clues.

Directions: Write something each character says in the left column. Then write your inferences about the characters on the right.

◄ Inference Chart

What the Character Says	My Inferences about the Character

Step 3: Look for clues about mood.

Writers often use dialogue to help establish mood.

Directions: Reread the information about dialogue and mood on page 356 of the *Reader's Handbook*. Then make an inference about the mood of the story.

I think the mood is .... because ....

....

....

Step 4: Look for clues about plot.

Sometimes what the characters say to themselves or others can give you clues about what's going to happen next in the plot.

Directions: Make a prediction of what will happen next in this story. Then explain your prediction.

My prediction: ....

....

I think this will happen because: ....

....

....

Focus on Comparing and Contrasting

Follow these steps when you are asked to compare a single literary element in two or more works.

Step 1: Read and make notes.

First, read both works. Then choose the literary element you want to compare and make a few notes.

Directions: Here are the opening paragraphs from two famous novels. Read each paragraph. Highlight words and phrases that catch your attention. Make notes on the stickies.

from *A Tale of Two Cities* by Charles Dickens

It was the best of times, it was the worst of times, it was the age of wisdom, it was the age of foolishness, it was the epoch of belief, it was the epoch of incredulity, it was the season of Light, it was the season of Darkness, it was the spring of hope, it was the winter of despair, we had everything before us, we had nothing before us, we were all going direct to Heaven, we were all going direct the other way—in short, the period was so far like the present period, that some of its noisiest authorities insisted on its being received, for good or for evil, in the superlative degree of comparison only.

from *The Garden of Eden* by Ernest Hemingway

They were living at le Grau du Roi then and the hotel was on a canal that ran from the walled city of Aigues Mortes straight down to the sea. They could see the towers of Aigues Mortes across the low plain of the Camargue and they rode there on their bicycles at some time of nearly every day along the white road that bordered the canal. In the evenings and the mornings when there was a rising tide sea bass would come into it and they would see the mullet jumping wildly to escape from the bass and watch the swelling bulge of the water as the bass attacked.

Dickens's words

are:

....

....

....

Hemingway's words

are:

....

....

....

Step 2: Organize.

Directions: Make notes about Dickens's and Hemingway's writing style on the Key Topic Notes organizer that follows.

NAME ....

Key Topic Notes

Key Topics	Text Notes
Dickens's words	
Dickens's sentences	
Hemingway's words	
Hemingway's sentences	

Step 3: Draw conclusions.

Finish by using a Venn Diagram to compare the two elements.

Directions: Complete the following organizer.

Venn Diagram

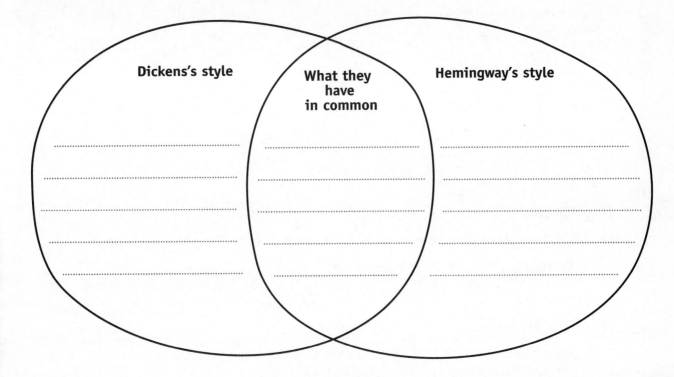

Dickens's style   What they have in common   Hemingway's style

Fiction

Reading a Poem

Poetry is often very artful. It can take a trained eye to understand it. Good readers know to examine every word and listen to every sound. Only then can they see and enjoy the finished "art" the poet has created.

Before Reading

Here you'll practice using the reading process and the strategy of close reading with a poem by the British poet Alfred, Lord Tennyson.

 ## A Set a Purpose

First, set your purpose. Remember that your end goal is to find out what the poem really means.

- **To set your purpose, ask questions about the subject, mood, and meaning of the poem.**

Directions: Write your purpose for reading "The Charge of the Light Brigade" below. Then make a prediction about the poem.

My purpose questions: ....

....

....

....

My prediction: ....

....

 ## B Preview

The purpose of your preview is to get a sense of what the poem is about.

Directions: Preview "The Charge of the Light Brigade." Write your preview notes on the lines below. Mark off each item on the Preview Checklist as you preview it.

NAME

Preview Checklist

- ☐ title
- ☐ background
- ☐ first line of poem
- ☐ overall shape of the poem
- ☐ last line of the poem

The title:

The poet's name:

From the background information I learned that:

The subject of the poem is:

I saw these repeated words and phrases:

Here's what I noticed about the shape and structure of the poem:

I noticed this about the rhyme scheme:

Background Information

The Crimean War (1850–1853) was a bloody conflict between Britain, France, and Russia. During this war, a group of 600 British soldiers (the Light Brigade) were mistakenly ordered to make a charge against the enemy. As a result, 247 of the 600 were killed or wounded.

Following the charge, Tennyson read an account of what happened in the newspaper. In the article, the reporter admitted that "someone had blundered." In a matter of minutes, an outraged Tennyson composed "The Charge of the Light Brigade," using "some one had blundered" to set the meter of the poem. It would become one of his most famous poems.

"The Charge of the Light Brigade" by Alfred, Lord Tennyson

I

Half a league, half a league,
    Half a league onward,
All in the valley of Death
    Rode the six hundred.
"Forward, the Light Brigade!
Charge for the guns!" he said:
Into the valley of Death
    Rode the six hundred.

II

"Forward, the Light Brigade!"
Was there a man dismay'd?
Not tho' the soldier knew
    Some one had blunder'd:
Their's not to make reply,
Their's not to reason why,
Their's but to do and die:
Into the valley of Death
    Rode the six hundred.

III

Cannon to right of them,
Cannon to left of them,
Cannon in front of them
    Volley'd and thunder'd;
Storm'd at with shot and shell,
Boldly they rode and well,
Into the jaws of Death,
Into the mouth of Hell
    Rode the six hundred.

IV

Flash'd all their sabres bare,
Flash'd as they turn'd in air
Sabring the gunners there,
Charging an army, while
    All the world wonder'd:
Plunged in the battery-smoke
Right thro' the line they broke;
Cossack and Russian
Reel'd from the sabre-stroke
    Shatter'd and sunder'd.
Then they rode back, but not
    Not the six hundred.

V

Cannon to right of them,
Cannon to left of them,
Cannon behind them
    Volley'd and thunder'd;
Storm'd at with shot and shell,
While horse and hero fell,
They that had fought so well
Came thro' the jaws of Death,
Back from the mouth of Hell,
All that was left of them,
    Left of six hundred.

VI

When can their glory fade?
O the wild charge they made!
    All the world wonder'd.
Honour the charge they made!
Honour the Light Brigade,
    Noble six hundred!

Plan

After your preview, choose a strategy that can help you understand and respond to the poem.

- **The strategy of close reading is the best strategy to use with poetry.**

During Reading

 D ## Read with a Purpose

Always plan on reading a poem several times. Think about a different aspect of the poem on each new reading.

Directions: Read "The Charge of the Light Brigade" several times. Make notes on this organizer.

Plan for Reading a Poem

First and Second Readings	Third and Fourth Readings	Fifth Reading
Here's what I liked about the poem:	This is what I noticed about the structure:	This is my reaction to the poem:
This is what I think the poet is saying:	This is the mood of the poem:	

Poetry

Using the Strategy

When you do a close reading, you read line for line, or even word for word.

• **Use a Double-entry Journal to keep track of your responses to individual lines and words in a poem.**

Directions: Read the lines from Tennyson's poem. Then write what the words mean or how they make you feel.

Double-entry Journal

Quote	Thoughts about it
"Their's not to make reply, Their's not to reason why, Their's but do and die:"	
"Cannon to right of them, Cannon to left of them, Cannon in front of them, Volley'd and thunder'd;"	
"Honour the charge they made! Honour the Light Brigade, Noble six hundred!"	

Understanding How Poems Are Organized

Many poems are organized around sound. In many cases, sound elements such as rhyme and rhythm are there to draw your attention to the underlying meaning of the poem.

Directions: Read "Rhyme and Rhyme Scheme" on page 438 of the *Reader's Handbook*. Use letters to mark the rhyme scheme of the first two stanzas from Tennyson's poem on page 152. Then answer the questions.

Who or what is the subject of this poem?
....

....

What is the mood?
....

Why do you think the poet repeats the phrase "the six hundred"?
....

....

E Connect

When you read a poem, try to connect it to your own life and experiences. This can make the poem easier to remember and talk about.

- **Connect to a poem by recording your thoughts and feelings about the sound and meaning of the work.**

Directions: Reflect on Tennyson's poem. Then complete these sentences.

◀ **Connection Comments**

When I read the poem, I felt:

....

....

....

I felt this way because:

....

....

....

Poetry

After Reading

F Pause and Reflect

Always give yourself a minute or two to reflect on what a poem means and whether or not you understood it.

- **After you finish a poem, ask yourself, "Have I answered my purpose questions?"**

Directions: Circle *have* or *have not*. Then explain your answer.

I feel I have/have not met my reading purpose. ....

Here's why: ....

....

....

....

....

Reread

Remember that an important part of reading a poem is enjoying it.

• **Use the rereading strategy of paraphrasing to help you reflect on your favorite lines from a poem.**

Directions: Choose three interesting lines or phrases from Tennyson's poem and record them on the left side of the chart. Then paraphrase the lines on the right.

Paraphrase Chart

Lines from the Poem	My Paraphrase
"Their's but to do and die"	
"Then they rode back, but not Not the six hundred."	
"O the wild charge they made!"	

 Remember

Before you leave a poem, try writing about it.

• **Writing can help you remember a poem's subject and meaning.**

Directions: Write a journal entry in which you describe "The Charge of the Light Brigade" and what it meant to you.

Journal Entry

....

....

....

....

NAME ....

Focus on Language

It's the way language is used that changes a poem from mere words on a page to a work of art. Your first step in understanding any poem is to listen—and respond to—the words and phrases the poet uses. Follow these steps.

Step 1: Read for key words.

On your first or second reading of a poem, watch for words that seem interesting or important. Keep an eye out for repeated words and words that are used outside of their normal, everyday meanings.

Directions: Read the following poem. Underline words that grab your attention. Then make notes on the stickies.

"The Lake Isle of Innisfree" by William Butler Yeats

I will arise and go now, and go to Innisfree,[1]
And a small cabin built there, of clay and wattles made:
Nine bean-rows will I have there, a hive for the honey bee,
And live alone in the bee-loud glade.

And I shall have some peace there, for peach come dropping slow,
Dropping from the veils of the morning to where the cricket sings;
There midnight's all a-glimmer, and noon a purple glow,
And evening full of the linnet's wings.

I will arise and go now for always night and day
I hear lake water lapping with low sounds by the shore;
While I stand on the roadway, or on the pavements gray,
I hear it in the deep heart's core.

_____

Innisfree—In Gallic, the word *Innisfree* means "Heather Island." In the second stanza, the speaker refers to the reflection of heather in the water with the phrase "noon a purple glow."

What is the subject of the poem?

....
....
....
....

How does the poet feel about the subject?

....
....
....

Poetry

Step 2: Think about word connotations.

Connotation is the feelings suggested by a word. Poets use connotation to establish mood and shape meaning.

Directions: Read the words from Yeats's poem on the left of the chart below. Write their connotations on the right.

Word Connotations

Words from the Poem	Feelings They Convey
honey bee, peace, peach, a-glimmer	
roadway, pavements gray	

Step 3: Look for figurative language, imagery, and repetition.

Good poets can make familiar words seem fresh and new. They do this through their use of figurative language, imagery, and repetition.

Directions: Look at these examples of imagery in "The Lake Isle of Innisfree" listed below. Tell what you picture and the senses you use.

Imagery Chart

Image in the Poem	What I Picture	The Sense or Senses I Use
"And live alone in the bee-loud glade."		
"There midnight's all a-glimmer, and noon a purple glow. "		
"And I shall have some peace there, for peach come dropping slow."		
". . . lake water lapping with low sounds by the shore."		

> If you need help with the terms *imagery, figurative language,* and *metaphor,* see "Elements of Poetry," pages 423–443 in your handbook.

NAME

Step 4: Examine the mood.

Poets use language to establish mood. The mood, in turn, can give you a feel for the underlying meaning of the poem.

Directions: Write a journal entry in which you discuss the mood of "The Lake Isle of Innisfree." Then explain what you think is the underlying meaning of the poem.

Journal Entry

The mood of the poem is:

....

....

....

....

....

....

....

....

....

I think the poem means:

....

....

....

....

....

....

....

....

Poetry

Focus on  Meaning

*Good poets can express a world of meaning in just a few
lines. Use the reading process to help you make inferences
about a poet's meaning and message for readers.*

Step 1: Examine the poem's language.

Use the strategy of close reading to examine individual words in the poem.

Directions: Read this part of a poem. Highlight words that you feel are
interesting or important. Then make notes on the stickies.

"After Death" by Christina Rossetti

The curtains were half drawn; the floor was swept
   And strewn with rushes; rosemary and may
   Lay thick upon the bed on which I lay,
Where, through the lattice, ivy shadows crept.
He leaned above me, thinking that I slept
   And could not hear him; but I heard him say,
   "Poor child, poor child"; and he has turned away
Came a deep silence, and I knew he wept.
He did not touch the shroud, or raise the fold
   That hid my face, or take my hand in his,
      Or ruffle the smooth pillows for my head.
      He did not love me living; but once dead
  He pitied me; and very sweet it is
To know he still is warm though I am cold.

What "death" words
did you find in the poem?

What is the effect
of these words?

NAME ....

FOR USE WITH PAGES 408–414

Step 2: Think about the poet's style.

Most poets use figurative language, imagery, rhyme, and rhythm to establish meaning.

Directions: Think about the style of Rossetti's poem. Then complete this Close Reading Organizer.

> **Close Reading Organizer**

Poem Text	My Thoughts
"Where, through the lattice, ivy shadows crept."	
"Came a deep silence, and I knew he wept."	

Step 3: Reflect on the poet's attitude.

Use this formula when exploring the underlying meaning of a poem:

Topic of the poem + What the poet is saying about the topic = The poet's message

Directions: Use the formula to find Rossetti's message in "After Death."

(Subject of the poem)   (What Rossetti says)   (The poet's message)

....   **+**   ....   **=**   ....

....

....

Step 4: Listen to your own feelings.

Ask yourself, "How does the poem make me feel?"

Directions: Write your feelings about Rossetti's poem.

The poem makes me feel .... because ....

....

Poetry

Focus on Sound and Structure

Focusing on how a poem looks and sounds can enhance your understanding of what it means. Follow these steps.

Step 1: Do a careful reading.

First, read a poem the whole way through without stopping. Then think about how it looks on the page and what it sounds like.

Directions: Read this stanza from "The Bells," a poem by Edgar Allan Poe. Then make notes on the stickies.

from "The Bells" by Edgar Allan Poe

Here the sledges with the bells—
Silver bells!
What a world of merriment their melody foretells!
How they tinkle, tinkle, tinkle,
In the icy air of night!
While the stars that oversprinkle
All the heavens, seem to twinkle
With a crystalline delight;
Keeping time, time, time,
In a sort of tunic rhyme,
To the tintinnabulation that so musically wells
From the bells, bells, bells, bells, bells,
Bells, bells, bells—
From the jingling and the tinkling of the bells.

What would you say the poem sounds like?

What do you notice about how this poem looks?

Which line attracts your attention most, and why?

What do you notice about the rhyme?

Step 2: Listen for repeated sounds.

After you examine the rhyme, listen to the sound of the poem. What are the words like? What effect do they create?

Directions: Look for examples of repetition, alliteration, and assonance in "The Bells." If you need help with these terms, see pages 418–419 in the *Reader's Handbook.*

Poetic Sounds Chart

Repeated words:	
Alliteration (repeated consonant sounds)	**Assonance** (repeated vowel sounds)

Step 3: Explore the rhyme scheme.

Poets use rhyme and rhythm for many reasons, including:

- to establish a mood

- to bring emphasis to an idea

- to enhance the reader's enjoyment

Directions: Read the second stanza of Poe's "The Bells." Then answer the rhyme and rhythm questions that follow.

Poetry

from "The Bells" by Edgar Allan Poe

II

Hear the mellow wedding bells—
Golden bells!
What a world of happiness their harmony foretells!
Through the balmy air of night
How they ring out their delight!—
From the molten-golden notes,
And all in tune,
What a liquid ditty floats
To the turtledove that listens, while she gloats
On the moon!
Oh, from out the sounding cells,
What a gush of euphony voluminously wells!
How it swells!
How it wells
On the Future!—how it tells
Of the rapture that impels
To the swinging and the ringing
Of the bells, bells, bells—
Of the bells, bells, bells, bells,
Bells, bells, bells—
To the rhyming and the chiming of the bells!

Rhyme and Rhythm Questions

What is the rhyme scheme in Poe's poem?

....

....

Does it change from stanza to stanza?

....

What is the meter of the poem?

....

How does Poe use meter to draw attention to the "bells" lines?

....

Reading a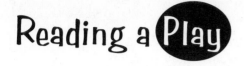

Plays are meant to be performed, but that doesn't mean that you can't enjoy reading them as well. The trick is to "listen" to what the characters say and visualize what they see.

Before Reading

The reading process and the strategy of summarizing can help you get more from a play. Practice here with an excerpt from *A Doll's House*, a famous play by Norwegian playwright Henrik Ibsen.

 A **Set a Purpose**

Your purpose for reading a play is to understand what happens and figure out what it means.

> • **To set your purpose, ask questions about the setting, characters, conflict, and theme of the play.**

Directions: Write your purpose for reading *A Doll's House* below. Then write what you already know about the play or the playwright.

My purpose questions:

....

....

....

....

What I already know:

....

....

....

....

Drama

B Preview

At the preview stage, focus your attention on the title page. Look for both setting and character clues. Try to get a sense of what the play is about.

Directions: Preview the title page for *A Doll's House*. Make notes on the stickies.

A Doll's House by Henrik Ibsen

DRAMATIS PERSONAE

Torvald Helmer.	Helmer's three young children.
Nora, his wife.	Anne, their nurse.
Doctor Rank.	A Housemaid.
Mrs. Linde.	A Porter.
Nils Krogstad.	

SETTING

Time: Christmas Eve, early 1900s

Place: Norway

The action takes place in Helmer's house.

(SCENE—*A room furnished comfortably and tastefully, but not extravagantly. At the back, a door to the right leads to the entrance-hall, another to the left leads to Helmer's study. Between the doors stands a piano. In the middle of the left-hand wall is a door, and beyond it a window. Near the window are a round table, arm-chairs, and a small sofa. In the right-hand wall, at the farther end, another door; and on the same side, nearer the footlights, a stove, two easy chairs and a rocking-chair; between the stove and the door, a small table. Engravings on the walls; a cabinet with china and other small objects; a small book-case with well-bound books. The floors are carpeted, and a fire burns in the stove. It is winter.*

—A bell rings in the hall; shortly afterward the door is heard to open. Enter NORA, *humming a tune and in high spirits. She is in outdoor dress and carries a number of parcels; these she lays on the table to the right. She leaves the outer door open after her, and through it is seen a* PORTER *who is carrying a Christmas tree and a basket, which he gives to the* MAID *who has opened the door.*)

The setting is
....
....

Number of
....
characters:

This is what I learned from the
title page:
....
....
....
....

Plan

After your preview, make a plan. Choose a strategy that can help you understand the characters, actions, and themes of the play.

- **Use the strategy of summarizing to help you keep track of important elements in a play.**

During Reading

D Read with a Purpose

A reading tool that works well with the strategy of summarizing is a Character Map.

Directions: Now do a careful reading of this scene from *A Doll's House*. Summarize your notes about Nora on this Character Map.

◀ **Character Map**

What the character says and does	What others think about the character

Nora

How the character acts and feels	How I feel about the character

Drama

from *A Doll's House* by Henrik Ibsen

NORA: Hide the Christmas Tree carefully, Helen. Be sure the children do not see it until this evening, when it is dressed. (*TO THE PORTER, TAKING OUT HER PURSE.*) How much?

PORTER: Sixpence.

NORA: There is a shilling. No, keep the change. (*THE PORTER THANKS HER, AND GOES OUT. NORA SHUTS THE DOOR. SHE IS LAUGHING TO HERSELF, AS SHE TAKES OFF HER HAT AND COAT. SHE TAKES A PACKET OF MACAROONS FROM HER POCKET AND EATS ONE OR TWO; THEN GOES CAUTIOUSLY TO HER HUSBAND'S DOOR AND LISTENS.*) Yes, he is in. (*STILL HUMMING, SHE GOES TO THE TABLE ON THE RIGHT.*)

HELMER (*CALLS OUT FROM HIS ROOM*): Is that my little lark twittering out there?

NORA (*BUSY OPENING SOME OF THE PARCELS*): Yes, it is!

HELMER: Is it my little squirrel bustling about?

NORA: Yes!

HELMER: When did my squirrel come home?

NORA: Just now. (*PUTS THE BAG OF MACAROONS INTO HER POCKET AND—WIPES HER MOUTH.*) Come in here, Torvald, and see what I have bought.

HELMER: Don't disturb me. (*A LITTLE LATER, HE OPENS THE DOOR AND LOOKS INTO THE ROOM, PEN IN HAND.*) Bought, did you say? All these things? Has my little spendthrift been wasting money again?

NORA: Yes but, Torvald, this year we really can let ourselves go a little. This is the first Christmas that we have not needed to economize.

HELMER: Still, you know, we can't spend money recklessly.

NORA: Yes, Torvald, we may be a wee bit more reckless now, mayn't we? Just a tiny wee bit! You are going to have a big salary and earn lots and lots of money.

HELMER: Yes, after the New Year; but then it will be a whole quarter before the salary is due.

Stop and Organize

What inferences can you make about Nora? Make notes on the Character Map on page 167.

NORA: Pooh! we can borrow until then.

HELMER: Nora! (*GOES UP TO HER AND TAKES HER PLAYFULLY BY THE EAR.*) The same little featherhead! Suppose, now, that I borrowed fifty pounds today, and you spent it all in the Christmas week, and then on New Year's Eve a slate fell on my head and killed me,—and—

NORA (*PUTTING HER HANDS OVER HIS MOUTH*): Oh! don't say such horrid things.

HELMER: Still, suppose that happened,—what then?

NORA: If that were to happen, I don't suppose I should care whether I owed money or not.

from *A Doll's House* by Henrik Ibsen

HELMER: Yes, but what about the people who had lent it?

NORA: They? Who would bother about them? I should not know who they were.

HELMER: That is like a woman! But seriously, Nora, you know what I think about that. No debt, no borrowing. There can be no freedom or beauty about a home life that depends on borrowing and debt. We two have kept bravely on the straight road so far, and we will go on the same way for the short time longer that there need be any struggle.

NORA *(MOVING TOWARDS THE STOVE)*: As you please, Torvald.

HELMER *(FOLLOWING HER)*: Come, come, my little skylark must not droop her wings. What is this! Is my little squirrel out of temper? *(TAKING OUT HIS PURSE.)* Nora, what do you think I have got here?

NORA *(TURNING ROUND QUICKLY)*: Money!

HELMER: There you are. *(GIVES HER SOME MONEY.)* Do you think I don't know what a lot is wanted for housekeeping at Christmas-time?

NORA *(COUNTING)*: Ten shillings—a pound—two pounds! Thank you, thank you, Torvald; that will keep me going for a long time.

HELMER: Indeed it must.

Stop and Organize

How does Helmer feel about Nora? Make notes on the Character Map on page 167.

NORA: Yes, yes, it will. But come here and let me show you what I have bought. And all so cheap! Look, here is a new suit for Ivar, and a sword; and a horse and a trumpet for Bob; and a doll and dolly's bedstead for Emmy,—they are very plain, but anyway she will soon break them in pieces. And here are dress-lengths and handkerchiefs for the maids; old Anne ought really to have something better.

HELMER: And what is in this parcel?

NORA *(CRYING OUT)*: No, no! you mustn't see that until this evening.

HELMER: Very well. But now tell me, you extravagant little person, what would you like for yourself?

NORA: For myself? Oh, I am sure I don't want anything.

HELMER: Yes, but you must. Tell me something reasonable that you would particularly like to have.

NORA: No, I really can't think of anything—unless, Torvald—

HELMER: Well?

NORA *(PLAYING WITH HIS COAT BUTTONS, AND WITHOUT RAISING HER EYES TO HIS)*: If you really want to give me something, you might—you might—

HELMER: Well, out with it!

NORA *(SPEAKING QUICKLY)*: You might give me money, Torvald. Only just as much as you can afford; and then one of these days I will buy something with it.

Drama

◁ **from _A Doll's House_ by Henrik Ibsen, continued** ▷

HELMER: But, Nora—

NORA: Oh, do! dear Torvald; please, please do! Then I will wrap it up in beautiful gilt paper and hang it on the Christmas Tree. Wouldn't that be fun?

HELMER: What are little people called that are always wasting money?

NORA: Spendthrifts—I know. Let us do as you suggest, Torvald, and then I shall have time to think what I am most in want of. That is a very sensible plan, isn't it?—

HELMER (_SMILING_): Indeed it is—that is to say, if you were really to save out of the money I give you, and then really buy something for yourself. But if you spend it all on the housekeeping and any number of unnecessary things, then I merely have to pay up again.

NORA: Oh but, Torvald—

HELMER: You can't deny it, my dear little Nora. (_PUTS HIS ARM ROUND HER WAIST._) It's a sweet little spendthrift, but she uses up a deal of money. One would hardly believe how expensive such little persons are!

NORA: It's a shame to say that. I do really save all I can.

HELMER (_LAUGHING_): That's very true,—all you can. But you can't save anything!

NORA (_SMILING QUIETLY AND HAPPILY_): You haven't any idea how many expenses we skylarks and squirrels have, Torvald.

Stop and Organize

How does Nora act in this scene? Make notes on the Character Map on page 167.

Using the Strategy

You can use a Magnet Organizer to explore the "big ideas" in a play. Very often the "big ideas" will point the way to one or more of the playwright's themes.

Directions: An important idea in _A Doll's House_ is "a woman's role in the family." Explore this idea on the Magnet Organizer on the next page. Then summarize your thoughts.

NAME _____

Magnet Organizer

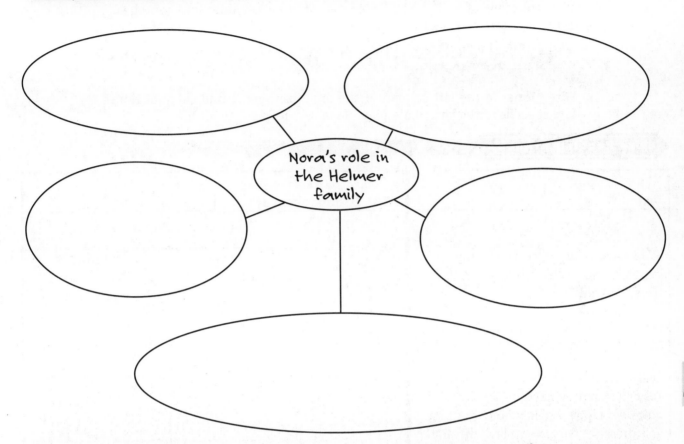

Nora's role in
the Helmer
family

Summary

....
....
....
....
....
....
....
....
....

Drama

Understanding How Plays Are Organized

In every scene of a play, you'll find one or more key lines and speeches. These can give you additional clues about the playwright's themes.

- **Use a Close Reading Organizer to help you respond to important lines and speeches in a play.**

Directions: In the left column of the organizer, you'll find three of Nora's key speeches from the whole play. Read and respond to each.

Close Reading Organizer

Text	What I Think about It
"You haven't any idea how many expenses we skylarks and squirrels have, Torvald."	
"[O]f course a time will come when Torvald is not as devoted to me, not quite so happy when I dance for him, and dress for him, and play with him."	
"I have been performing tricks for you, Torvald. That's how I've survived. You wanted it like that. You and Papa have done me a great wrong. It's because of you I've made nothing of my life."	

 Connect

Thinking about your reactions and connections to a play can sharpen your understanding of the playwright's themes. It can help you think more critically about what you've read.

- **Connect to a play by recording your thoughts and feelings about the characters and action.**

NAME ....

FOR USE WITH PAGES 447–468

Directions: Reread this piece of dialogue from *A Doll's House*. Then write your reaction.

> HELMER *(FOLLOWING HER)*: Come, come, my little skylark must not droop her wings. What is this! Is my little squirrel out of temper? *(TAKING OUT HIS PURSE.)* Nora, what do you think I have got here?
>
> NORA *(TURNING ROUND QUICKLY)*: Money!
>
> HELMER: There you are. *(GIVES HER SOME MONEY.)* Do you think I don't know what a lot is wanted for housekeeping at Christmas-time?
>
> NORA *(COUNTING)*: Ten shillings—a pound—two pounds! Thank you, thank you, Torvald; that will keep me going for a long time.
>
> HELMER: Indeed it must.

My reaction: ....

....

....

After Reading

F   Pause and Reflect

When you finish a play, think about what you've learned. Ask yourself about the characters, setting, conflict, and theme.

• **Always check to see if you've met your original reading purpose.**

Directions: How well did you meet your reading purpose? What would you like to find out more about? Explain here.

....

....

....

G   Reread

Remember that a part of your job is to visualize what the characters in a play are "seeing."

• **A powerful rereading strategy to use is visualizing. It can help you "see" important ideas in the play.**

Directions: Draw a portrait of Nora. Then write a caption that explains your thoughts about her.

◄ Sketch

Caption:

H Remember

If you read the play for a school assignment, you'll need to find a way to remember what you read.

• **Doing an oral reading of a key scene can help you recall important elements of the play.**

Directions: Choose a short passage from *A Doll's House*. Then get together with a partner and read your scenes aloud. Discuss why you chose this particular passage.

Passage from *A Doll's House* ....

....

....

....

....

....

....

....

....

Why I chose this passage: ....

....

NAME ....

Focus on Language

The language of a play drives the action. For this reason, it is vitally important that you "listen" to what the characters are saying and think about how they are saying it.

Step 1: Examine key lines and speeches.

On your first reading of a play, keep an eye out for key lines and speeches. They can reveal important clues about a character.

In the speech from *A Doll's House* below, Nora reveals that she once borrowed money from a stranger in order to have enough for Helmer, who was desperately sick, to travel to Italy and be cured.

Directions: Read what Nora says. Note any words used to describe her. Then write your thoughts about her personality on the sticky note.

from *A Doll's House* by Henrik Ibsen

NORA: But it was absolutely necessary that [Helmer] should not know! My goodness, can't you understand that? It was necessary he should have no idea what a dangerous condition he was in. It was to me that the doctors came and said that his life was in danger, and that the only thing to save him was to live in the south. Do you suppose I didn't try, first of all, to get what I wanted as if it were for myself? I told him how much I should love to travel abroad like other young wives; I tried tears and entreaties with him; I told him that he ought to remember the condition I was in, and that he ought to be kind and indulgent to me; I even hinted that he might raise a loan. That nearly made him angry, Christine. He said I was thoughtless, and that it was his duty as my husband not to indulge me in my whims and caprices—as I believe he called them. Very well, I thought, you must be saved—and that was how I came to devise a way out of the difficulty.

Words that describe Nora:
....
....
....
....

My inferences about her:
....
....
....
....
....

Drama

Step 2: Read the stage directions.

Also pay careful attention to the stage directions. Remember that one of the reasons a playwright gives stage directions is to help readers visualize a scene.

Directions: Reread the stage directions from the opening of Act I of *A Doll's House* (see page 166). Then read these stage directions, which come from the opening of Act II. Make notes on the lines below.

> **from *A Doll's House* by Henrik Ibsen**
>
> (SCENE—*The Christmas tree is in the corner by the piano, stripped of its ornaments and with burnt-down candle-ends on its disheveled branches. NORA'S cloak and hat are lying on the sofa. She is alone in the room, walking about uneasily. She stops by the sofa and takes up her cloak.*)

This is what I noticed about the stage directions for Act I:

....

....

This is what I noticed about the stage directions for Act II:

....

....

....

Step 3: Analyze the dialogue.

As a final step, analyze the conversations between the characters. Keep in mind that dialogue can point the way to a play's theme.

Directions: In the piece of dialogue on the next page, Helmer reacts to Nora's news that she is leaving him. Read the dialogue and then make notes on the Double-entry Journal.

NAME ....

from *A Doll's House* by Henrik Ibsen

HELMER: All over! All over!—Nora, shall you never think of me again?

NORA: I know I shall often think of you, the children, and this house.

HELMER: May I write to you, Nora?

NORA: No—never. You must not do that.

HELMER: But at least let me send you—

NORA: Nothing—nothing—.

HELMER: Let me help you if you are in want.

NORA: No. I can receive nothing from a stranger.

HELMER: Nora—can I never be anything more than a stranger to you?

NORA *(TAKING HER BAG)*: Ah, Torvald, the most wonderful thing of all would have to happen.

HELMER: Tell me what that would be!

NORA: Both you and I would have to be so changed that—. Oh, Torvald, I don't believe any longer in wonderful things happening.

HELMER: But I will believe in it. Tell me! So changed that—?

NORA: That our life together would be a real wedlock. Goodbye.

(SHE GOES OUT THROUGH THE HALL.)

Double-entry Journal

Quote	My Thoughts
HELMER: All over! All over!—Nora, shall you never think of me again?	
NORA: Both you and I would have to be so changed that—. Oh, Torvald, I don't believe any longer in wonderful things happening.	
NORA: That our life together would be a real wedlock. Goodbye.	

Focus on Theme

The theme of a play is the playwright's message for the audience. Good plays will have several themes, although one usually is more important than the others. Use this three-step plan to interpret a playwright's theme.

Step 1: Find the general topics.

First, find the major ideas, or general topics, in a play. Ask yourself, "What people, places, things, and ideas is this play about?"

Directions: Think about repeated words and ideas in *A Doll's House.* Write them on the Web below.

Web

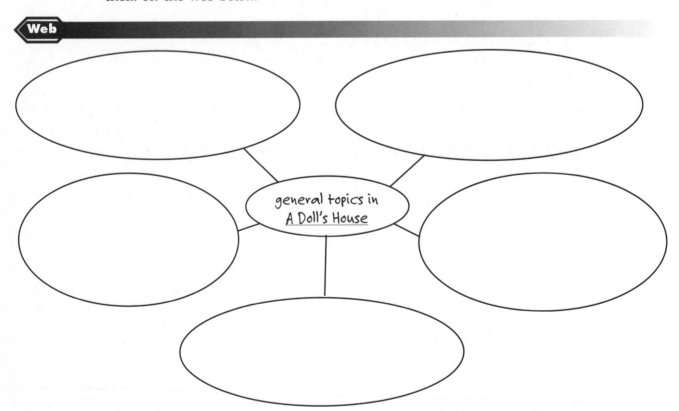

general topics in
A Doll's House

Step 2: Note what the characters say and do.

Next, think about what the characters say and do that relate to these general topics.

Directions: Choose one general topic from your Web to explore on the organizer on the next page.

General Topic:

What Nora Says and Does	What Helmer Says and Does

Step 3: Write a theme statement.

Theme is the playwright's message about the general topic.

Directions: Read the information about finding a theme on pages 483–484 in the *Reader's Handbook*. Then explore one of Ibsen's most important topics in *A Doll's House:* marriage.

Theme Organizer

Drama

Topic: Marriage

Detail #1:

Detail #2:

Detail #3:

Theme:

Focus on Shakespeare

Follow these steps when reading a play by Shakespeare.

Step 1: Read for sense.

Your first step is to understand what is being said.

Directions: Reread pages 485–489 of the *Reader's Handbook*. Then read this famous courtroom scene from Shakespeare. Write your thoughts on the sticky notes.

from *The Merchant of Venice* by William Shakespeare

DUKE: Make room, and let him stand before our face.
    Shylock, the world thinks, and I think so too,
    That thou but leadest this fashion of thy malice
    To the last hour of act; and then, 'tis thought,
    Thou'lt show thy mercy and remorse, more strange
    Than is thy strange apparent cruelty;
    And where thou now exacts the penalty,—
    Which is a pound of this poor [Antonio's] flesh,—
    Thou wilt not only loose the forfeiture,
    But, touch'd with human gentleness and love,
    Forgive a moiety of the principal,
    Glancing an eye of pity on his losses,
    That have of late so huddled on his back,
    Enow to press a royal merchant down,
    And pluck commiseration of his state
    From brassy bosoms and rough hearts of flint,
    From stubborn Turks and Tartars, never train'd
    To offices of tender courtesy.
    We all expect a gentle answer, Jew.
SHYLOCK: I have possess'd your Grace of what I purpose,
    And by our holy Sabbath have I sworn
    To have the due and forfeit of my bond.
    If you deny it, let the danger light
    Upon your charter and your city's freedom.
    You'll ask me why I rather choose to have
    A weight of carrion flesh than to receive
    Three thousand ducats. I'll not answer that,
    But say it is my humour: is it answer'd?

This is what the Duke is saying:
....
....
....
....

This is Shylock's response:
....
....
....
....
....

Step 2: Read for specifics.

Next, make inferences about characters, plot, and theme.

Directions: Read the text on the left. Then record your thoughts.

◀ **Inference Chart**

Text	What it tells me about the character
Thou'lt show thy mercy and remorse, more strange Than is thy strange apparent cruelty;	
You'll ask me why I rather choose to have A weight of carrion flesh than to receive Three thousand ducats. I'll not answer that, But say it is my humour: is it answer'd?	

Step 3: Reflect.

As a final step, reflect on what the play meant to you.

Directions: Think about your experiences with reading Shakespeare. Record your comments on the lines below.

When I read Shakespeare, I enjoy

....

....

....

What I find challenging is the   because

....

....

....

Drama

Reading a **Website**

You can find a wealth of information on the Internet, but not all of it is factually correct. This is why it's so important that you read every website with a critical eye.

Before Reading

Use the reading process and the strategy of reading critically with a website designed for movie buffs.

A **Set a Purpose**

It's pretty easy to get lost on the Internet. To prevent this from happening, set your purpose *before* you go to a website. This is particularly important if you're visiting the site for a school assignment.

> **• To set your purpose, make a list of questions about the subject.**

Directions: Imagine your assignment is to review a website called moviemania.com for your school newspaper. Write three or more purpose questions here.

Purpose Questions

....

....

....

....

....

B Preview

Always preview a site before you begin navigating through it. Figure out what the site offers and how you will use it to meet your purpose.

Directions: Preview the movie buffs website that follows. Look at each item on this checklist. Make notes about what you find.

Preview Checklist

Preview Checklist	My Notes
❑ the name and overall look of the site	
❑ the main menu or table of contents	
❑ the source or sponsor	
❑ any descriptions of the site	
❑ any images or graphics that create a feeling	
❑ the purpose of the site	

Internet

http://www.moviemania.movies.com/home.asp

Subscribers log in here

The National Movie Society Presents . . .

Moviemania.com

Moviemania.com has information on the movies you want to see!
Check our listings for films playing now, or search our archives
for films of the past.

SEARCH by Movie or Person

Local Showtimes and Tickets

Select a movie

Can't find your movie?

Movie Reviews

Link to reviews of today's
hottest films.

The New York Times

The Wall Street Journal

Newsweek

Hollywood.com

Moviegoers are talking about . . .

Cannes
Independent Film Festivals
Studio Mergers

click here for more
on these subjects

Check Out Our Film Archives!
We offer information on 1000s of movies, plus all award-winners
for the past 100 years.

About our Archives
Best Picture   Best Actress   Best Actor   Best Director   Best Screenplay

Moviemania.com is a project of the National Movie Society, an affiliate of Bear Creek University in Bear Creek, New York.
Dr. Lila Jackson, Chairperson of the Department of Film Production at Bear Creek University, is the director of this site.
Direct your comments to Dr. Jackson at www.ljackson@nms.com. To learn more about the National Movie Society, visit their
home page at www.nationalmoviesociety.com.

This site is updated daily. Last updated: August 29, 2003

C Plan

Next, plan how to best meet your purpose. Use the strategy of reading critically to help you read and evaluate the website.

• **Reading critically means asking yourself, "How much can I trust the information on this website?"**

During Reading

D Read with a Purpose

Remember that your main purpose in reading a website is to find reliable information that you can use.

<u>Directions:</u> Read the movie website carefully. Write your notes on this Website Profiler.

Website Profiler

URL	
Sponsor	Date
Point of view	Expertise
Reaction/Evaluation	

Internet

Using the Strategy

Study Cards can help you keep track of your research questions and the key facts you learn about from the website.

- **Remember to read critically each new link you follow from the original site.**

Directions: Make notes about the movie buffs website on these study cards. Tell which links you should follow and explain why.

Study Cards

What links should I follow?

How well does the site address my purpose?

Notes about www.moviemaniamovies.com

Keep your note cards in front of you as you link to other sites.

Understanding How Websites Are Organized

A website really does resemble a Web. The "spokes" that reach out from the center are the links you can follow for additional information.

Directions: Complete this Web. List three important links on the movie buffs website. Make a prediction about what you think you'll find at each link.

Web

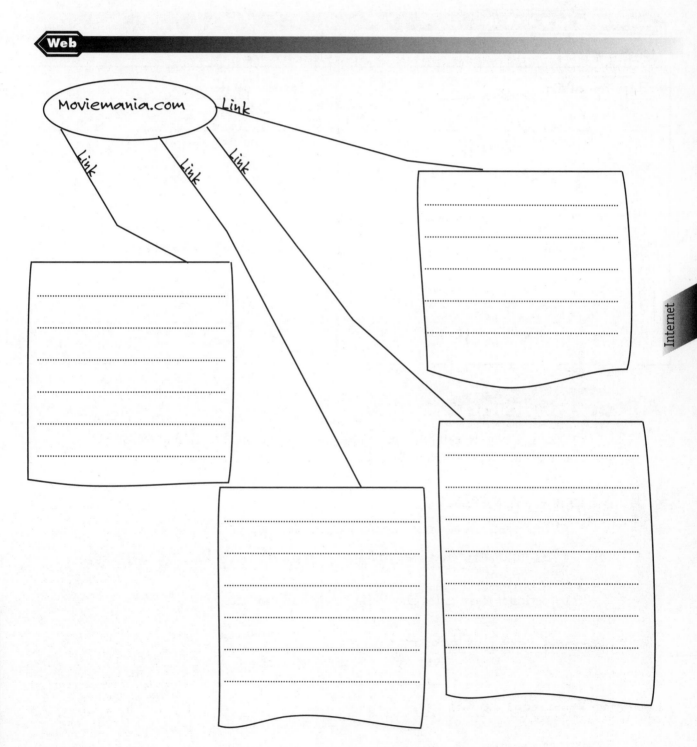

Internet

Connect

When you connect to a website, you consider whether the site was helpful and if you'd like to return.

- **Be sure to consider whether the website was of use to you personally.**

<u>Directions:</u> Think of two websites you've visited recently. Explain your opinion of each site and why you will or will not return.

◄ **Connecting to a Website**

Website #1	Website #2
My opinion of it:	My opinion of it:
Why I will or will not return:	Why I will or will not return:

After Reading

Take the time to carefully examine what you see on the original website before moving on to another one.

 Pause and Reflect

At this point, recall your original purpose for visiting the site.

- **Ask yourself, "How well did I meet my purpose? What else do I need to find out?"**

<u>Directions:</u> Make notes about the movie buffs website here.

What I learned from this website:

....

....

I want to know more about:

....

....

Reread

If you're not sure how reliable a website is, do some rereading.

• **Use the rereading strategy of skimming when checking the reliability of the information posted on a site.**

Directions: Skim the movie buffs website. Then answer the "reliability" questions below.

Evaluating Internet Sources

1. What is the source of the site?

2. What credentials does the site offer?

3. What is the primary purpose of the site?

4. Does it meet that purpose?

5. When was the site last updated?

6. Are there any obvious errors or omissions on the site?

 Remember

Recording information about a website on a graphic organizer can help you remember it.

• **Use a graphic organizer to help you process and remember key elements of a website.**

Directions: Complete this organizer using information from the movie buffs website.

Source Evaluator

Research purpose	
Source type	Date
Title or location	
Expertise	
Bias, if any	

Internet

Reading a Graphic

Graphics are word pictures; they are a visual representation of information. When you read a graphic, work first to understand the information the graphic presents and then think carefully about what it means.

Before Reading

Use the reading process and the strategy of paraphrasing to help you read and respond to a graphic about changes in the number of vehicles in U.S. households.

 A **Set a Purpose**

Two specific questions can help you set your purpose when reading a graphic: *What is the graphic about?* and *What does it mean?*

> • **To set your purpose, ask questions about the content and meaning of a graphic.**

Directions: Write your purpose questions for reading a bar graph that compares number of vehicles in U.S. households in 1990 and in 2000. Then make a prediction.

Purpose question #1: ....

....

Purpose question #2: ....

....

My prediction: ....

....

....

 B **Preview**

At the preview stage, try to get a sense of the "big picture" shown in the graphic.

Directions: Preview the bar graph on the next page. Then make some preview notes.

NAME

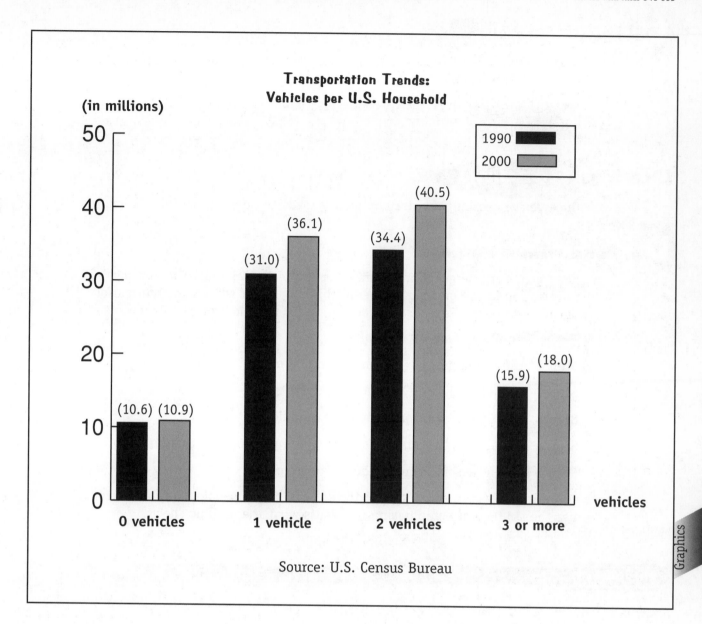

Transportation Trends:
Vehicles per U.S. Household

(in millions)

1990
2000

50

40

(40.5)

(36.1)

(31.0)   (34.4)

30

20

(18.0)

(15.9)

(10.6) (10.9)

10

0

0 vehicles   1 vehicle   2 vehicles   3 or more   vehicles

Source: U.S. Census Bureau

Graphics

Title of the graphic:

Type of graphic:

Dates represented:

Labels, column headings, and row headings:

What is the big picture?

Plan

Next, make a plan. Choose a strategy that will help you read, interpret, and respond to the graphic.

• **The strategy of paraphrasing can help you process key facts and details.**

During Reading

Once you've chosen your strategy, you're ready to do your careful reading.

D **Read with a Purpose**

Keep your purpose questions in mind as you read. Make notes about key information in the graphic and begin thinking about what that information means. Review the *Reader's Handbook* plan for reading a graphic below.

Plan for Reading a Graphic

Step 1 Scan the graphic to get an impression of the "big picture."

Step 2 Read all of the text, including any captions.

Step 3 Tell in your own words what the graphic shows.

Step 4 Think about the quality, meaning, and purpose of the information.

Step 5 Make a personal connection to the graphic.

Directions: Read carefully the "Vehicles per U.S. Household" graphic. Then use the strategy of paraphrasing to discuss what the graphic shows.

Paraphrase

What the "Vehicles per U.S. Household" graphic shows:

....

....

....

....

What the information means:

....

....

....

....

Using the Strategy

Paraphrasing can help you process and remember what you've read.

Directions: Complete the Paraphrase Chart using information from the "Vehicles per U.S. Household" graphic. See page 549 of the *Reader's Handbook* if you're not sure how to use this tool.

Paraphrase Chart

Title	
My Paraphrase	
My Thoughts	

Graphics

Understanding How Graphics Are Organized

Familiarize yourself with the vocabulary of graphics. Key terms include *source, x axis,* and *y axis.*

Directions: Label the following elements on the graphic below: *title, source, horizontal (x) axis,* and *vertical (y) axis.* Then answer the questions to be sure that you really understand the data that is being presented.

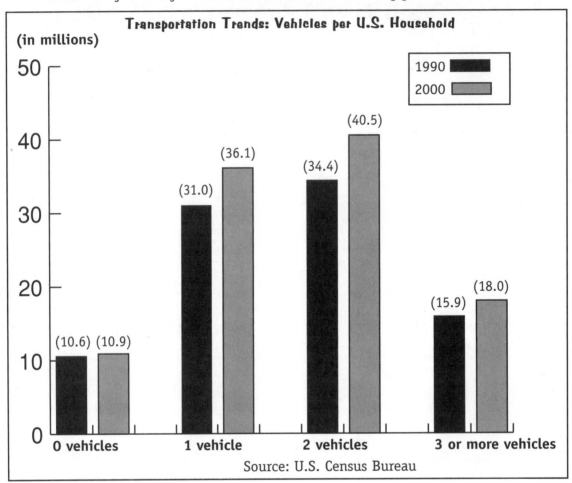

How many U.S. households owned 2 vehicles in 1990?

How many owned 2 vehicles in the year 2000?

What do you notice about households owning 0 vehicles?

What do you predict would be the total number of households with 1 vehicle in the year 2010?

Explain.

Connect

Connecting to a graphic means asking yourself, "What does this information mean to me?" or "How does this information change my view of the world?"

• **Making a personal connection to a graphic can help you better understand and remember the information that is being presented.**

Directions: Record your thoughts about the vehicles per household graphic on this Double-entry Journal.

Double-entry Journal

Graphic	My Thoughts

After Reading

 Pause and Reflect

Always take a second (or third) look at a graphic before leaving it altogether.

• **Ask yourself, "How well did I meet my purpose for reading?"**

Directions: Answer your reading purpose questions.

What is the graphic about?

....

....

What does it show me?

....

....

Reread

A part of your job when reading any type of nonfiction (including graphics) is to question whether the information is true.

• **Use the rereading strategy of reading critically to help you decide whether the information in a graphic is valid.**

Directions: Take another look at the vehicles per household graphic. Then complete this Critical Reading Chart.

Critical Reading Chart

"Transportation Trends: Vehicles per U.S. Household"	
1. What is being compared?	
2. What similarities do I see?	
3. What differences do I see?	
4. Is there anything unusual about the way the data is presented?	
5. What trends or other relationships do I see?	

Remember

Your handbook suggests two techniques you can use to remember the information presented in a graphic. A third technique is to create your own graphic of the same information. This can help you process what you've learned.

• **Redrawing a graphic can help you more easily remember the information presented.**

Directions: Review the Transportation Trends graphic shown on page 191. Then create your own graphic that presents the same information in a different way.

> **Possible Graphics to Use**
>
> Line graph
>
> Pie graph
>
> Bar graph
>
> Table or chart
>
> Diagram
>
> Map

Graph

Graphics

Reading a Driver's Handbook

In some cases, reading carefully can save your life. This is certainly true for reading a driver's handbook. Use the reading process and critical thinking strategies to help you process and remember the information.

Before Reading

Use the reading process and the strategy of skimming to help you read and respond to a state driver's handbook.

A Set a Purpose

Your purpose for reading a driver's handbook is twofold: to learn the rules of the road in your state and to prepare for the written examination to get a driver's permit.

- **To set your purpose, ask questions about the material you're about to read.**

Directions: Write three purpose questions for reading a driver's handbook. Then make predictions about the text.

My purpose questions:

1. ....

2. ....

3. ....

My predictions:

I think the easiest parts of a driver's handbook will be

....

....

I think the most challenging parts will be

....

....

NAME ....

 B **Preview**

During your preview, find out as much as you can about the topic of the chapter.

Directions: Preview the chapter from a driver's handbook. Make notes on the stickies.

Chapter 7: Passing Another Vehicle

In general, it is the law that you drive on the right side of the road. When passing is permitted, you must pass other vehicles on the left. Passing on the right is permitted only under special circumstances and should be done with extreme caution. It's important to note that you must *not* exceed the speed limit to pass another vehicle.

You are required by law to use directional or hand signals when passing another vehicle. You must indicate your desire to pass at least 100 feet before making your lane change.

Under no circumstances may you pass a vehicle that has stopped at a crosswalk so as to allow a pedestrian or group of pedestrians to cross.

Passing on the Left

On most roads, the left lane is intended for passing other vehicles. However, you may NOT pass a vehicle on the left if:

1. Your lane has a solid yellow center line.
2. You cannot safely return to the right lane before reaching a solid yellow center line for the right lane.
3. You cannot safely return to the right lane before any type of approaching vehicle comes within 200 feet of you.
4. You are on a curve.
5. You are within 100 feet of a railroad crossing.
6. You are within 100 feet of a bridge or tunnel.
7. Passing will in any way jeopardize the safety of your vehicle or other vehicles on the roadway.

> If you determine conditions for passing are ideal, follow these steps:
>
> - Check your mirrors.
> - Signal your lane change.
> - Do a full over-the-shoulder check.

When passing, move completely into the left lane. Once your vehicle is entirely in the left lane, check your mirrors and then over your shoulder to be certain that you can see the front bumper of the vehicle you've passed. Then return to the right-hand lane.

Everyday

Chapter 7: Passing Another Vehicle, continued

Passing on the Right

As discussed above, you usually will pass other vehicles on the left. Passing on the right is only allowed in certain circumstances. You may pass on the right if:

1. A vehicle ahead of you is making a left-hand turn.
2. You are driving on a one-way road that is marked for two or more lanes and passing is not restricted by signs.

When passing on the right at an intersection, always take a careful look at the traffic ahead of you. Make sure an oncoming vehicle is not turning left into your path. Be alert for pedestrians, bicyclists, in-line skaters, and moped or scooter riders.

If you are passing on the right on a multilane road such as an expressway, follow these steps:

1. Check your mirrors.
2. Turn on your directionals or perform the correct hand signals.
3. Complete a full over-the-shoulder check.

After passing, check over your left shoulder and signal before returning to the right lane.

What I learned from the headings:

Boldface terms I noticed:

I also noticed:

C Plan

Most critical readers find that the strategy of skimming can help them get *more* from a driver's handbook.

> • Skimming can help you zero in on key facts and details.

Many reading tools work well with the strategy of skimming. Thumb through pages 575–577 of the *Reader's Handbook* and find a reading tool that you can use consistently to help you with the strategy of skimming.

During Reading

 Read with a Purpose

Remember your purpose for reading: to learn the rules of the road and prepare for your state driving examination.

Directions: Read this chapter from a driver's handbook. Make notes on the Key Word or Topic Notes below.

Key Word or Topic Notes

Key Word or Topic	Notes
passing other vehicles	
passing on the left	
passing on the right	
using directionals or hand signals	
Over-the-shoulder checks	

Everyday

Using the Strategy

Skimming is a strategy that works before, during, and after reading.

Directions: Make notes on these Study Cards. Create more cards on a separate sheet of paper or on other notecards of your own.

Study Cards

Rules for passing

another vehicle

Over-the-shoulder

checks

When you can

pass on the right

NAME ....

 Connect

Make a connection between what you read and your own life.

> **• Visualizing how you'll apply the information in a driver's handbook can help you remember it.**

Directions: Use this Storyboard to show how to pass on the left. Write a caption under each sketch.

◄ **Storyboard**

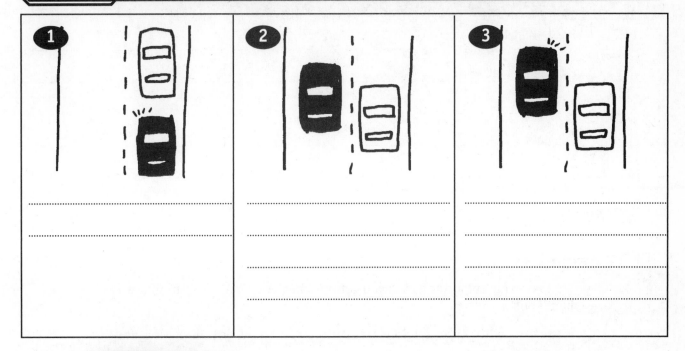

After Reading

F **Pause and Reflect**

After you finish the driver's handbook, ask yourself, "Have I learned what I need to know?"

> **• Return to your original purpose and reflect on what you've learned.**

Directions: Answer these questions about the chapter you just read.

◄ **Looking Back**

1. What is important for you to remember about passing another vehicle? ....

....

....

2. What do you need to find out more about? ....

....

Everyday

Reread

You may need to reread key parts or all of a driver's handbook before you take your test.

• **A powerful rereading strategy to use with real-world writing is visualizing and thinking aloud.**

Directions: Write a Think Aloud in which you explain how to pass on the right.

Think Aloud

....

....

....

....

....

Remember

It's extremely important that you retain what you've learned from a driver's handbook.

• **Asking "what if" questions about key facts and details for a good memory aid.**

Directions: Answer these "What if" questions. Then write two of your own.

Questions

1. What if you need to pass a car that is stopped for pedestrians?

....

2. What if you are on a one-way highway with two lanes? Is it all right to pass on the right?

....

3. My question:

....

4. My question:

....

Focus on Reading Instructions

You read instructions at school, at work, and at home. Here are steps to follow when the instructions are particularly important or particularly confusing.

Step 1: Set your purpose.

You'll naturally have a purpose in mind before you pick up the instructions. Think about this purpose as you preview the text. Mark the parts that you know you need to read.

Directions: What would your purpose be for reading instructions on how to start a lawn mower? Write it here.

My purpose: ....

....

Step 2: Read carefully.

Next, begin reading. Mark important words and phrases.

Directions: Read the set of instructions that follows. Highlight the most important details.

Starting/Stopping Your Mower

Before starting the engine on your mower, read the entire set of directions that follows.

Warning: Mishandling of this product can result in serious injury.

1. FILL THE FUEL TANK TO THE "F" LINE. If fuel is low, mower will not start.
2. Put the IGNITION SWITCH IN THE "ON" POSITION.
3. FULLY PRESS AND RELEASE THE PRIMER BULB 5 TO 7 TIMES.
    Pressing more than 7 times may cause engine flooding.
4. PLACE THE CHOKE LEVER IN THE "FULL CHOKE" POSITION.
5. PULL THE STARTER ROPE BRISKLY 1 TO 3 TIMES TO START ENGINE.
6. If engine does not start, repeat steps 4 and 5.
7. After the engine warms up for 5 to 10 seconds, PLACE THE CHOKE LEVER IN THE "RUN" POSITION.
8. To stop the engine, put the IGNITION SWITCH IN THE "OFF" POSITION.

Everyday

Step 3: Think aloud.

It can help to think aloud as you read and follow the instructions.

Directions: Write a Think Aloud that describes the steps involved in starting your mower.

◄ Think Aloud ▬▬▬▬▬▬▬▬▬▬▬▬▬▬▬▬▬▬▬▬▬▬

....

....

....

....

....

....

....

....

....

Step 4: Ask questions.

Asking questions can help you carry out the steps discussed in the instructions. If you're not sure of a step, ask yourself a question about it. This will give you another way to think through the information.

Directions: Write a question about Steps 3 and 7 of the mower instructions.

My question about step 3: ....

....

My answer: ....

....

My question about step 7: ....

....

My answer: ....

NAME ....

Focus on Reading for Work

Reading is an important part of any after-school job. When you finish school and begin your career, your ability to read critically will become even more essential. The reading process can help.

Step 1: Identify your purpose.

Not all workplace reading is relevant—that is, important to you. Before you read a workplace document, be sure you understand your purpose.

Directions: On the page that follows, you'll find a sick leave policy for a retail company. Imagine you are an employee of this company. Note your purpose in reading the policy below.

My purpose: ....

....

Step 2: Understand how the writing is organized.

Next, preview the text to see how it is organized. This will make it easier to find the information you need.

Directions: Preview the sick leave policy statement on the next page. Make notes on this Preview Chart.

◄ **Preview Chart**

What is the subject of the policy statement?	Who wrote it?
(Sick Leave Policy)	
When was it written?	For whom was it written?

Everyday

207

Sick Leave Policy

Value Department Stores, Inc.
325 West 87th Street
New York, New York 10103
November 2002

FROM THE HUMAN RESOURCES DEPARTMENT
SICK LEAVE POLICY

Purpose:

To establish the sick leave policy in effect at Value Department Stores, Inc., and to define the terms under which employees can be paid for their sick leave.

Policy:

It is the policy of the company that each full-time employee is eligible for paid sick leave pending the approval of his or her supervisor.

Specifically:

- All employees working thirty (30) or more hours per week are eligible for paid sick leave.
- Eligibility for paid sick leave begins with the date of hire.
- The sick leave plan allows for unlimited accrual. As a result, employees may build a substantial level of protection against serious illness if they so choose.
- The weekly accrual rate is equal to one (1) hour of sick leave for every forty (40) hours worked.
- Regardless of the number of hours worked, sick leave is not paid until the employee has completed two (2) full months of service.
- Absences resulting from work-related injuries or illnesses will be compensated under the State Worker's Compensation and shall not be charged against the employee's sick leave accrual.
- Accrued sick leave balances lapse upon the termination of employment.
- If the nature of the illness requires sick leave for more than five (5) days, a signed note from a licensed physician must be presented to a supervisor for approval. No payment for sick leave beyond day five (5) will be made without a signed doctor's note. See Absenteeism Policy.

This policy applies to
....
....
....

The bulleted list
tells me
....
....

What is the purpose of the
fifth item?
....
....
....
....

NAME ....

Step 3: Find out what you need to know.

Use the strategy of skimming to find the information you need in a workplace document. Pay particular attention to bulleted lists and words in boldface or italics.

Directions: Now go back and do a careful reading of the sick leave policy on page 208. Highlight key words and phrases. Make notes on the stickies.

Step 4: Apply the information to your own life.

When you've finished reading, figure out how the information applies to you. Then find a way to remember it.

Directions: Reflect on the sick leave policy you just read. In the space below, list the most important points and how they would affect you if you were an employee of Value Department Stores, Inc.

From the desk of

Sick Leave Policy at Value Department Stores

Everyday

Reading Tests and Test Questions

The reading process can help you read, interpret, and answer any type of test question.

Before Reading

Preparing beforehand is essential to performing well on a test. When you are given the test, you'll begin by setting your purpose. During the test itself, you'll use the strategy of skimming to help you answer each question.

A   Set a Purpose

No matter what type of test you take, your purpose is this: figure out what the test questions are asking and then decide how to answer them.

• **To set your purpose, ask questions about the test and test questions.**

Directions: For this sample test, you'll read a short excerpt from a novel called *Krik? Krak!* by Edwidge Danticat. Write your purpose questions here.

My purpose questions: ....

....

....

....

....

....

....

....

B   Preview

Once you've set your purpose, preview the test. Try to get a sense of what the questions are like.

Directions: Preview the sample test that follows. Write your thoughts on the sticky notes.

Mid-Year Reading Test

30 Minutes—4 Questions, 1 Essay

DIRECTIONS: Circle the letter of the correct answer to each question. You will not be penalized for incorrect answers. Write your essay in the blue test booklet.

MID-YEAR READING TEST, PASSAGE #1

I have to complete the test.

from *Krik? Krak!* by Edwidge Danticat

We spent most of yesterday telling stories. Someone says, Krik? You answer, Krak! And they say, I have many stories I could tell you, and then they go on and tell these stories to you, but mostly to themselves. Sometimes it feels like we have been at sea longer than the many years that I have been on this earth. The sun comes up and goes down. That is how you know it has been a whole day. I feel like we are sailing for Africa. Maybe we will go to Guinin[1], to live with the spirits, to be with everyone who has come and has died before us. They would probably turn us away from there too. Someone has a transistor and sometimes we listen to radio from the Bahamas, a woman says. To them, we are not human. Even though their music sounds like ours. Their people look like ours. Even though we had the same African fathers who probably crossed these same seas together.

[1] Guinin—a peaceful land where gods and goddesses live. In Haitian lore, the body's spirit goes to Guinin after death.

Mid-year Reading Test

Passage #1 Multiple-choice Questions

1. From what point of view is *Krik? Krak!* told?
   A. objective
   B. third-person limited omniscient
   C. first-person
   D. third-person omniscient

From the title, I predict the reading will be about:

2. What is Krik? Krak!?
   A. a story request
   B. the names of two characters
   C. an old Haitian prayer
   D. a word game

I learned this from the directions:

Tests

Mid-Year Reading Test

Someone has a transistor and sometimes we listen to radio from the Bahamas, a woman says.

3. What is a synonym for the word *transistor* as it is used in the sentence above?

    A. television   C. radio

    B. harmonica   D. transmitter

I noticed this about the test questions:

4. What is the setting for this scene from *Krik? Krak?*

    A. present day in the Bahamas   C. present day on a boat

    B. a long time ago in Africa   D. present day on an airplane

5. What would you say is the narrator's chief emotion in this scene?

    A. regret   C. bitterness

    B. anger   D. fright

6. Why do you think these people are on the boat?

    A. They are going deep sea fishing.   C. They were forced to leave their homeland.

    B. They are making their way to Africa.   D. They are going back home to Haiti.

Essay Question

7. Explain what you think the author means by the phrase "They would probably turn us away from there too." Use details from the excerpt to support what you say.

C Plan

Because most tests require you to return to the passage or problem again and again, you'll need to find a strategy that can help you read quickly and process information as you go.

- **Skimming can help you find the answers you need in the shortest amount of time.**

Notice that in this test-taking plan skimming plays an important role.

Test-taking Plan

Step 1 Read the passage or problem.

Step 2 Read the questions and look for key words.

Step 3 Skim the passage for those key words.

Step 4 Once you find the key words in the passage, read the sentence before and after that.

Step 5 Then look back and try to answer the test questions.

During Reading

 Read with a Purpose

Keep your purpose in mind when reading the passage. Read slowly, and make notes as you go.

Directions: Now read the excerpt from *Krik? Krak!* Underline important words or phrases. Then summarize the passage here.

Summary

....

....

....

....

....

....

....

....

Using the Strategy

Once you've read the passage, you can begin answering the questions. Read each question. Skim the passage for answers.

Directions: Read the six multiple-choice questions on pages 211–212. Highlight key words in each. Then tell where you should skim to find the answers.

Question #	Where I'll Begin Skimming
1	
2	
3	
4	
5	
6	

Tests

Understanding How Tests Are Organized

Usually the most challenging questions will appear at the end of the test.

Directions: Reread questions 5 and 6. Then explain which words and sentences in the reading help you answer them.

5. What would you say is the narrator's chief emotion in this scene?
   A. regret
   B. anger
   C. bitterness
   D. fright

Clues I found:

The narrator's chief emotion is

6. Why do you think these people are on the boat?
   A. They are going deep sea fishing.
   B. They are making their way to Africa.
   C. They were forced to leave their homeland.
   D. They are going back home to Haiti.

Clues I found:

Why do you think these people are on the boat?

NAME ....

E Connect

Connecting to a test means thinking about how the passage or problem relates to your own life. Considering how you yourself might handle the situation or solve a problem can help you understand a character's thoughts and feelings.

- **A question like "How would *I* feel in this situation?" can help you make a quick connection to a test passage.**

<u>**Directions:**</u> Reread the essay question. Then complete the sticky note.

Essay Question

7. Explain what you think the author means by the phrase "They would probably turn us away from there too." Use details from the excerpt to support what you say.

If I were the narrator, I would feel:

....

....

....

....

After Reading

F Pause and Reflect

Reserve at least a few minutes at the end of the test to check your work. Are there any questions that you skipped or answers that need work?

- **Remember your reading purpose: to find out what the test questions are asking and figure out what information is needed to answer them.**

<u>**Directions:**</u> Answer these questions about the sample test.

Pause and Reflect Questions

Which question did you think was easiest? Why? ....

....

....

Which did you find most challenging? Why? ....

....

....

....

Tests

Reread

Use the strategy of visualizing and thinking aloud to help you answer questions that are difficult for you.

- **Visualizing and thinking aloud can help you more clearly "see" the answer to a question.**

Directions: Reread the essay question on page 212. Then write a Think Aloud that tells how you would answer it.

Think Aloud

H **Remember**

After your teacher grades your test, reread any questions you got wrong. Think about how you *should have* answered the questions.

- **Make note of the test questions that you found difficult. They might show up again on another exam.**

Directions: Exchange books with a partner and grade each other's tests. Be sure to comment on your partner's Think Aloud. Then explain what you could do to improve your test-taking abilities.

I can improve my test-taking abilities by

Focus on English Tests

Most exams in English class test your knowledge of vocabulary, grammar, usage, and mechanics. In addition, there may be one or more reading components. Following the reading process and taking time to study some of the major rules of grammar, usage, and mechanics can help you.

Step 1: Read the questions.

After your preview, read the questions one at a time. Mark the most important words in each.

Directions: Read the questions on this sample test. Highlight the most important words.

◁ Sample Test ▷

Part 1 Vocabulary

1. If GRAT means "pleasing," what does ingrate mean?

   A. highly pleased   B. not pleased   C. constantly pleased   D. seldom pleased

2. If FIG means "form," what does disfigure mean?

   A. create   B. disagree   C. ruin   D. reform

Part 2 Grammar

Use the sentence below to answer questions 3 and 4.

   Stop that car!

3. What is the subject of the sentence?

   A. stop   B. car   C. you   D. they

4. The sentence above is an example of a/an _____ sentence.

   A. exclamatory   B. interrogative   C. imperative   D. declarative

Part 3 Usage and Mechanics

   My sister and _____ visited a museum last year.

5. Choose the word that correctly completes the above sentence.

   A. I   B. us   C. me   D. them

6. Which of the following sentences is not punctuated correctly?

   A. Two girls and one boy visited my house yesterday.

   B. I'll have a hamburger, fries and a glass of milk.

   C. Will you bring me a fork, spoon, and napkin?

   D. Determined to see inside the crate, Shawan pried up one of the boards.

Step 2: Eliminate incorrect answers.

Next, read over every answer choice. Eliminate those you know are wrong.

Directions: Read the answer choices for each sample question. Cross out as many incorrect answers as you can.

Step 3: Use test-taking strategies.

To answer vocabulary questions, use such word strategies as searching for context clues. If you get stuck, talk yourself through the question.

Directions: On the lines below, explain how to figure out the correct answer for each of the six questions.

To answer question #1, I need to
....

....

To answer question #2, I need to
....

....

....

To answer question #3, I need to
....

....

....

To answer question #4, I need to
....

....

....

To answer question #5, I need to
....

....

....

To answer question #6, I need to
....

....

....

Step 4: Figure out word relationships.

Save word analogy questions for last because they can be tricky. To solve an analogy, figure out how the given word pair is related. Then find another pair within the answer choices that has the same relationship.

Directions: Read these sample questions. Then write your thoughts on the sticky notes.

Part 4 Word Analogies

7. shroud : veil ::
   A. flour : cake
   B. dupe : trick
   C. grass : green
   D. merciless : sympathetic

8. worst : wurst ::
   A. avarice : generosity
   B. your : you're
   C. magnet : magnate
   D. discomfort : embarrassment

9. learn : school ::
   A. plane : pilot
   B. pencil : book
   C. swimming : hiking
   D. shopping : mall

How shroud and veil are related: _____

_____ The correct answer is ____ because _____

How worst and wurst are related: _____

The correct answer is because _____

How learn and school are related: _____

The correct answer is because

Tests

Focus on Writing Tests

The writing and the reading processes go hand in hand. Use both processes together on your next writing test.

Step 1: Read the directions and prompt.

With an essay question on a test, always begin by reading the directions or prompt. Figure out the type of essay you're to write and what the topic is supposed to be.

Directions: Read the sample directions and prompt below. Underline key words and phrases. Then organize your thoughts on the sticky notes.

Sample Test

PROMPT: A wealthy alumnus has offered to donate money to your school for a new library or gymnasium. Students have been asked to vote on how the money should be used.

DIRECTIONS: Write a letter to the editor of the school newspaper in which you give your opinion on how the money should be spent and persuade readers to adopt your viewpoint. Remember to fully explain your argument and offer at least three supporting details. Be sure to proofread your work when you've finished.

The topic of the essay:

....

The type of essay I'm to write:

....

What I need to do to write the essay:

1. ....

2. ....

3. ....

4. ....

Step 2: Write an opinion or thesis statement.

Your next step is to write your opinion or thesis statement. This will be the controlling idea of your essay.

Directions: Use the formula to write an opinion statement for the library vs. gymnasium issue.

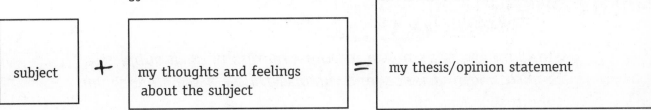

subject + my thoughts and feelings about the subject = my thesis/opinion statement

Step 3: Organize.

Next, make a writing plan. Use a Main Idea Organizer to help.

Directions: Plan the gym or library essay on this organizer.

Main Idea Organizer

My opinion:		
Detail 1	**Detail 2**	**Detail 3**

When you write an essay, use a combination of personal details and details from other sources, such as facts, figures, and examples.

Step 4: Write and then proofread.

Put your thesis or opinion statement in the introduction.

Directions: Write the introductory paragraph for the gym vs. library essay. Proofread carefully.

....

....

....

Tests

Focus on Standardized Tests

Standardized tests measure your progress in such subjects as English, math, science, and history. Follow these steps when taking this type of exam.

Step 1: Read the directions.

Always listen to the verbal directions and read carefully the written directions.

Directions: Read these sample test directions. Underline key words.

> **Sample Test**
>
> **DIRECTIONS:** Mark only one answer to each question. You will NOT be penalized for wrong answers, so it is in your best interest to answer every question on the test, even if you must make a guess. When you've finished with a section, close your book. Do NOT move on to the next section until you are told to do so.

Step 2: Read the questions.

Read the questions one at a time. Try to think of an answer before reading the answer choices given.

Directions: Read this sample question. Write your thoughts on the sticky note.

> **Sample Test**
>
> 7. The Food and Drug Administration rejected the new diet drug because they found that it caused _____ side effects.

The question is asking me to

Key words in the question are:

Step 3: Read the answers.

Next, read every possible answer to the question, even if you're sure you know the correct one. Eliminate answers that are clearly wrong.

Directions: Read the five possible answers to the diet drug question. Eliminate answers that are clearly wrong. Write your thoughts on the sticky note.

Sample Test

1. The Food and Drug Administration rejected the new diet drug because they found that it caused _____ side effects.
   A. award-winning
   B. irresponsible
   C. worrisome
   D. dynamic
   E. invigorating

I can eliminate answers because

Step 4 : Make an educated guess.

If you absolutely do not know the correct answer, use the strategy of thinking aloud to help you make an educated guess.

Directions: Write a Think Aloud in which you explain the correct answer to the diet drug question. Explain how you arrived at the answer.

Think Aloud

Focus on History Tests

Reading critically is an important part of succeeding on a history test. Follow this four-step plan.

Step 1: Read the question.

After your preview, begin reading the questions. Mark the key words.

Directions: Read the sample questions. Highlight the most important words, and then make notes on the sticky.

> ### Sample Questions
>
> 1. The "Black Death" is a nickname for:
>   A. World War I
>   B. United States slavery
>   C. the Bubonic Plague
>   D. the Inquisition
>
> 2. A group of cities whose boundaries have extended to meet each other is called
>   A. a plurality
>   B. the suburbs
>   C. a metropolis
>   D. a megalopolis

To answer this question, I need to

To answer this question, I need to

Step 2: Rule out incorrect answers.

Next, read every answer choice, even if you're sure you know the answer. Eliminate incorrect answers as you go.

Directions: Return to the sample questions. Cross out answers that are clearly wrong. Then make notes on the lines below.

The answer to question 1 is _____ I know this because _____

....

....

The answer to question 2 is   . I know this because ....

....

....

....

....

....

Step 3: **With graphics, look at the "big picture."**

You may want to leave graphics questions for last, since these are often the most challenging. With each new graphic, ask yourself, "What can this graphic tell me?"

Directions: Study this graphic. Then read the question. Write your thoughts on the sticky note.

> **Sample Question**
>
> **Causes**
>
> 1. The French government, which was controlled by a king and his court, was bankrupt.
>
> 2. The Third Estate, or the common people, was forced to carry much of the tax burden.
>
> 3. The National Assembly was formed to break from the king and form a constitutional government.
>
> 4. _____
>
> **Effect**
>
> The French Revolution

Tests

⬡ **Sample Question**

3. Which of the following could serve as number 4 on the organizer on the previous page?

    A. Napoleon Bonaparte demanded change.

    B. Food was scarce, and the peasants were starving.

    C. Terrible fires had swept through most of France, leaving millions homeless.

    D. The Catholic Church ordered the French king to resign.

The "big picture" shown in this

graphic:

What I need to do to answer the

question:

Step 4: Talk through the answers.

If you don't know the answer to a question, use the strategy of thinking aloud.

Directions: Take a second look at the French Revolution graphic. Then write a Think Aloud that tells how you'd answer the question.

⬡ **Think Aloud**

FOR USE WITH PAGES 643–649

Focus on Math Tests

You might be surprised at how much reading you have to do on a math test. The reading process can help.

Step 1: Read the questions.

As always, preview a math test before you begin answering the questions. Take note of the key word or words in each question. Answer the easy questions first.

Directions: Read the questions on this sample test. Highlight key words in each.

Sample Test

1. Nana Janet's famous brownie recipe calls for 1/2 cup oil and 2 cups of chocolate chips per 36 bars. For the bake sale, she needs to make 144 bars. How many cups of oil and chocolate chips will she need for the bake sale?

   A. 1 cup oil, 3 cups of chips
   B. 2 cups oil, 8 cups of chips
   C. 1 1/2 cups oil, 6 cups of chips
   D. 4 cups oil, 8 cups of chips

2. During the final week of camp, nine campers went hiking on Monday, eleven campers went hiking on Tuesday, six went on Wednesday, and four went on both Thursday and Friday. What was the daily average of campers hiking this week at camp?

   A. 9
   B. 7
   C. 5
   D. 3

Step 2: Eliminate wrong answers.

Next, read the answer choices and eliminate those that are clearly wrong.

Directions: Return to the sample test. Cross out the answers you know are wrong.

Tests

Step 3: Estimate.

If you can, estimate the answer. Check to see if there is an answer that is close to your estimate.

Directions: Look at Question 1 again. Then estimate how many cups of oil and chips Nana Janet will need.

I estimate that it will take _____ cups of oil and _____ cups of chips. The answer is ....

Step 4: Visualize.

If you get stuck, try to visualize what the problem is saying.

Directions: Make a sketch to go with Question 2. Then write an equation to solve the problem.

....

....

....

Step 5: Check.

As a final step, check your work. Use a different method to solve the same problem.

Directions: In column 1, write a different way to solve the first sample test question. In column 2, write a different way to solve the second.

Equation 1	Equation 2

Focus on Science Tests

On any science test, you'll need to use the three R's: reading, recalling, and reasoning.

Step 1: Answer the easy questions.

As a first step, preview the test. Then read and answer one question at a time. Begin with the easiest ones first.

Directions: Read the question. Then write what you learned on the sticky note.

Science Test

1. What is physiology?
   A. The study of mental health
   B. The study of life processes in living things
   C. The study of muscles and the skeleton
   D. The study of the brain and nervous system

To answer the question, I need to

My answer is

Step 2: Answer the harder questions.

After you finish the easy questions, begin with the more challenging ones. Use the strategy of eliminating incorrect answers and thinking aloud.

Directions: Read this question and the answer choices. Eliminate those you know are wrong. Then write your thoughts on the sticky.

Science Test

2. The solid part of Earth's crust is called the
   A. atmosphere
   B. biosphere
   C. lithosphere
   D. hemisphere

Tests

Step 3: Answer the graphics questions.

To answer a graphics question, you must be able to extract information from the graphic and then decide what it means.

Directions: Examine this diagram and the two questions. Then write a Think Aloud that tells how you would answer them.

◤ **Graphics Question**

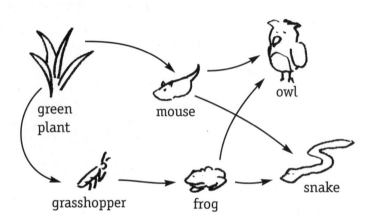

green plant

mouse

owl

grasshopper

frog

snake

DIRECTIONS: Use the diagram to answer questions 3 and 4.

3. Which of the items shown in the web is a producer? _____

4. Which is an omnivore? _____

◤ **Think Aloud**

....
....
....
....
....
....
....
....

Learning New Words

Good readers are word collectors. They gather new words as they read, and they practice using them after closing the book.

Step 1: Read.

Keep an eye out for unfamiliar words as you read. Your goal is to learn what the words mean and then make them your own.

Making New Words Your Own

1. List challenging words in a vocabulary journal.

2. Try defining new words in context as you read.

3. Use a dictionary whenever necessary.

4. Pronounce difficult words as you read.

5. Learn new words every day.

6. Use the new words in your writing and conversation.

For additional tips, see page 660 of your *Reading Handbook*.

Directions: Read the following paragraph from a novel. Circle any unfamiliar words.

from *Fahrenheit 451* by Ray Bradbury

It was a pleasure to burn.

It was a special pleasure to see things eaten, to see things blackened and *changed*. With the brass nozzle in his fists, with this great python spitting its venomous kerosene upon the world, the blood pounded in his head, and his hands were the hands of some amazing conductor playing all the symphonies of blazing and burning to bring down the tatters and charcoal ruins of history. With his symbolic helmet numbered 451 on his stolid head, and his eyes all orange flame with the thought of what came next, he flicked the igniter and the house jumped up in a gorging fire that burned the evening sky red and yellow and black. He strode in a swarm of fireflies. He wanted above all, like the old joke, to shove a marshmallow on a stick in the furnace, while the flapping pigeon-winged books died on the porch and lawn of the house, while the books went up in sparkling whirls and blew away on a wind turned dark and burning.

Vocabulary

Step 2: Record.

Keep a running record of words that are new to you.

Directions: Record unfamiliar words from the *Fahrenheit 451* excerpt in the journal below. Also write down the sentences or phrases in which you found the words.

Vocabulary Journal

from *Fahrenheit 451* by Ray Bradbury
Unfamiliar words
1.
Definition:
2.
Definition:
3.
Definition:
4.
Definition:

Step 3: Define.

Next, define each word.

Directions: Look up the unfamiliar words you listed and write down what they mean in the Vocabulary Journal.

Step 4: Use.

The best way to remember a word you've collected is to use it in conversation or in your writing.

Directions: Choose three of the words you listed above and write sentences for each.

My Sentences

....

....

....

FOR USE WITH PAGES 666-676

Skills for Learning New Words

There are other ways to figure out the meaning of a word besides checking a dictionary. These include using context clues and word parts.

Step 1: Use context clues.

When you come to an unfamiliar word, try defining it by its context. This means checking the text that surrounds the word to see if you can find clues about the unfamiliar word's meaning.

Directions: Read this excerpt from J. R. R. Tolkien's novel *The Return of the King*. Use context clues to figure out the meanings of the underlined words.

From *The Return of the King* by J. R. R. Tolkien

Pippin looked out from the shelter of Gandalf's cloak. He wondered if he was awake or sleeping, still in the swift-moving dream in which he had been wrapped so long since the great ride began. The dark world was rushing by and the wind sang loudly in his ears. He could see nothing but the wheeling stars, and away to his right vast shadows against the sky where the mountains of the South marched past. Sleepily he tried to reckon the times and stages of their journey, but his memory was drowsy and uncertain.

There had been the first ride at terrible speed without a halt, and then in the dawn he had seen a pale gleam of gold, and they had come to the silent town and the great empty house on the hill. And hardly had they reached its shelter when the winged shadow had passed over once again, and men wilted with fear. But Gandalf had spoken soft words to him, and he had slept in a corner, tired but easy, dimly aware of comings and goings and of men talking and Gandalf giving orders.

Underlined Words	My Definition	Context Clues I Used
vast		
reckon		
wilted		

Vocabulary

Step 2: Use word parts.

If you can't find context clues, check to see if there are any familiar word parts—root words, prefixes, or suffixes.

Root Word

Directions: In this scene from Tolkien's novel, Gandalf feels drowsy and "uncertain." Consider the *cert*, which means "determine." Then use what you've learned to define the words written in the tree.

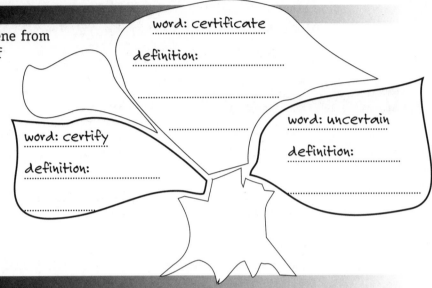

word: certificate

definition: ....

....

word: certify

definition: ....

....

word: uncertain

definition: ....

....

Prefixes

If you know the meaning of the prefix, you have a clue about the meaning of the whole word.

Directions: Add a prefix from the box to each of the words on the list. Then tell what the new word means.

ir- = not   *anti-, ant- = against*   *mis- = incorrect, bad*

Prefix + Word	New Word	Meaning of New Word
1. + *regular*		
2. + *acid*		
3. + *take*		

Suffixes

When you add a suffix to the end of a word, you change its meaning and usually its part of speech. Suffixes can also give you clues about an unfamiliar word's meaning.

-ology = study of   *-ence = action, state of, or quality of*   *-ful = full of*

1. bio   +   =   Meaning: ....

2. vigil   +   =   Meaning: ....

3. fright +   =   Meaning: ....

Dictionary Dipping

When you read for school, do so with a dictionary at your side. Then, when you come to a word you can't define in context, you can follow these steps.

Step 1: Read.

First, find the entry for the unfamiliar word. Then read it carefully.

Directions: Read this sample entry. Then answer the questions.

> **Dictionary**
>
> **junket** (jŭng′kĭt) *n.* **1.** A dessert made from flavored milk and rennet. **2.** A party or outing. **3.** A trip taken by a public official or businessperson at public or corporate expense. [ME *joonket,* rush basket.] —**jun′ket** *v.* — **jun′keter** *n.*

What part of speech is *junket?*

What is another noun form of *junket?*

Which syllable is stressed in *junket?*

How many definitions does the word *junket* have?

Step 2: Remember.

Then use the word in a sentence of your own. This can help you remember it.

Directions: Write a sentence for *junket* and another for *junketer.*

Sentence #1

Sentence #2

Vocabulary

235

Focus on Using a Thesaurus

Can't think of the perfect word? A thesaurus can help. Follow these steps when using a thesaurus.

Step 1: Read.

First, find the entry for the word in question. Then read the entire entry carefully.

Directions: Read the following entry. Then answer the questions.

> **Thesaurus**
>
> **victory,** *n.* conquest, triumph, success, mastery, supremacy, ascendancy, achievement, advantage, exultation, celebration, subjugation, masterstroke, walkover —*Ant.* defeat, retreat, rout, disaster.

What part of speech is *victory?*

Which synonym would you use to describe victory on the athletic field?

Which would you use to describe victory in a sculpture contest?

What are two antonyms for *victory?*

Step 2: Remember.

Using the synonyms for a word will help you remember them.

Directions: Use synonyms for *victory* to complete these phrases.

1. A stunning

2. The artist's

3.   over the team

NAME

Analogies

Solving analogies takes practice. The trick is to carefully study the relationship between the given words. Then you look for a word pair that explores that same relationship.

Step 1: Analyze the original pair.

First, figure out the relationship between the given pair of words. Make notes as needed.

Directions: Read the sample analogies. Write your thoughts on the sticky notes.

> **Sample Analogies**

1. jelly bean : candy ::
   A. Easter : Passover
   B. rabbit : animals
   C. fish : ocean
   D. purple : lilacs

How jelly bean and candy are related:

2. web : spider ::
   A. tiny : big
   B. bread : baker
   C. stop sign : policeman
   D. fly : mosquito

How web and spider are related:

3. arm : leg ::
   A. leaf : stem
   B. calm : frenzied
   C. sweet : sour
   D. climb : hill

How arm and leg are related:

4. dry : sky ::
   A. nature : environment
   B. pickle : dill
   C. fear : near
   D. book : pages

How dry and sky are related:

Vocabulary

Step 2: Explore the possible answers.

First, eliminate any answers that are clearly wrong. Then explore the word pairs that remain. The strategy of thinking aloud can help.

Directions: Return to the sample analogies. Cross out any answers that are clearly wrong. Then write Think Alouds to show how you decided on the correct answer.

Think Aloud

To answer Analogy 1, I need to

To answer Analogy 2, I need to

To answer Analogy 3, I need to

To answer Analogy 4, I need to

Step 3: Study.

When it comes time to study for a test that will contain analogies, begin by memorizing the most common types.

Directions: Reread pages 685–689 in the *Reader's Handbook*. Then write an example for each type of analogy listed below. Write examples that are different from the ones in your book.

Relationships in Analogies

1. Synonyms

   stout : heavy :: ....

2. Antonyms

   flippant : deferential :: ....

3. Parts of a Whole (Whole and Part)

   star : constellation :: ....

4. Item and What It Is Designed to Do (Is Used To)

   rule : measure :: ....

5. Item and Who Uses It

   calculator : mathematician :: ....

6. Action and Where It Takes Place (Is a Place Where)

   tours : museum :: ....

7. Result and Who Does It (Is Done By)

   cloth : weaver :: ....

8. Two Examples from the Same Class (Class and Subclass)

   insect : ladybug :: ....

9. Name and a Word that Describes It

   goat : ornery :: ....

10. Sequence

    chrysalis : butterfly :: ....

11. Different Forms of the Same Word

    buy : bought :: ....

12. Item and a Word That Describes It

    sandpaper : rough :: ....

Vocabulary

Author/Title Index

A

"After Death" (Rossetti), 160

B

"The Bells" (Poe), 162, 164

Bradbury, Ray, *Fahrenheit 451*, 231

Bulfinch, Thomas, "Pegasus and the Chimaera," 137

Burroughs, Edgar Rice, *Tarzan of the Apes*, 125, 127–132

C

"The Charge of the Light Brigade" (Tennyson), 152

Chekhov, Anton, "Rothschild's Fiddle," 17

"Child Labor and Women's Suffrage" (Kelley), 107–108

Cobb, Irvin S., "When the Sea-Asp Stings," 95, 97–100

Cooney, Caroline B., *Driver's Ed*, 15–16

D

Danticat, Edwidge, *Krik? Krak!*, 211

"Death of a Traveling Salesman" (Welty), 139

Dickens, Charles, *A Tale of Two Cities*, 148

A Doll's House (Ibsen), 166, 168–170, 175–177

Driver's Ed (Cooney), 15–16

DuBois, W. E. B., "Let Us Reason Together" from *The Crisis*, 66–67

E

Eastman, Charles A., *Spotted Tail*, 85, 87–89

F

Fahrenheit 451 (Bradbury), 231

G

The Garden of Eden (Hemingway), 148

"The Golden Honeymoon" (Lardner), 146

Golding, William, *Lord of the Flies*, 143

H

Hemingway, Ernest, *The Garden of Eden*, 148

Hsiu, Ou-Yang, "Pleasure Boat Studio," 59–60

I

Ibsen, Henrik, *A Doll's House*, 166, 168–170, 175–177

K

Kelley, Florence, "Child Labor and Women's Suffrage," 107–108

Krik? Krak! (Danticat), 211

L

"The Lake Isle of Innisfree" (Yeats), 157

Lardner, Ring, "The Golden Honeymoon," 146

"Let Us Reason Together" (DuBois), 66–67

Lord of the Flies (Golding), 143

M

Mansfield, Katherine, "The Voyage," 111–118

The Merchant of Venice (Shakespeare), 180

Morrison, Toni, *Song of Solomon*, 141

P

"Pegasus and the Chimaera" (Bulfinch), 137

"Pleasure Boat Studio" (Hsiu), 59–60

Poe, Edgar Allan, "The Bells," 162, 164

R

Return of the King, The (Tolkien), 233

Rossetti, Christina, "After Death," 160

"Rothschild's Fiddle" (Chekhov), 17

S

Shakespeare, William, *The Merchant of Venice*, 180

Song of Solomon (Morrison), 141

Spotted Tail (Eastman), 85, 87–89

T

A Tale of Two Cities (Dickens), 148

Tarzan of the Apes (Burroughs), 125, 127–132

Tennyson, Alfred, Lord, "The Charge of the Light Brigade," 152

"Two Inmates Vanish from Alcatraz," 76–78

Tolkien, J. R. R., *The Return of the King*, 233

V

"The Voyage" (Mansfield), 111–118

W

Welty, Eudora, "Death of a Traveling Salesman," 139

"When the Sea-Asp Stings," (Cobb), 95, 97–100

Y

Yeats, William Butler, "The Lake Isle of Innisfree," 157

Photo Credits